The
Presley
Family
Cookbook

*featuring recipe favorites
of the Presley family*

by
Vester Presley
and
Nancy Rooks

First Printing...........................1980
Second Printing......................1981
Third Printing..........................1982
Fourth Printing 1983
Fifth Printing...........................1985
Sixth Printing..........................1987
Seventh Printing....................1988
Eighth Printing.......................1989
Ninth Printing 1990
Tenth Printing........................1991
Eleventh Printing 1992
Twelfth Printing 1994
Thirteenth Printing................1995
Fourteenth Printing...............1998
Fifteenth Printing..................2003
Sixteenth Printing.................2006
Seventeenth Printing.............2009
Eighteenth Printing...............2010
Nineteenth Printing...............2011
Twentieth Printing 2012

Editor: Jane M. Coward
Artist: Dickey L. Stafford

International Standard Book Number – 978-0-918544-50-6

WIMMER
cookbooks
A CONSOLIDATED GRAPHICS COMPANY
wimmerco.com   800.548.2537

To Elvis Aaron Presley
   Vernon Elvis Presley
   Gladys Smith Presley
   Minnie Mae Presley

About
the
Authors

Vester Presley was born in Tupelo, Mississippi. He is married to Clettes Smith Presley and they have one child, Patsy Presley Gambill. Vester has been the guard at Graceland for over 23 years. He was very close to both his brother, Vernon Presley, and his nephew, Elvis. Vester is known affectionately as "Uncle Vester" to the many Elvis fans who still visit Graceland.

Nancy Rooks has been a maid and cook at Graceland since May, 1967. She is still employed there today. Nancy says, "We all loved our boss and his family. His home was like my own home because I spent more time there than at my house. He always said 'Thank you' when we served him. At times Mr. E.P. might put a $100.00 bill into my pocket and smile and say 'Don't say anything!' But I would thank him anyway. I always enjoyed preparing his food."

TABLE OF CONTENTS

Appetizers, Sandwiches, and Accompaniments

CHEESE BALL

¼ pound bleu cheese
½ pound cream cheese
1 pound sharp Cheddar
    cheese

1 teaspoon onion juice
⅓ cup pineapple juice
2 ounces chopped pimento
½ cup chopped parsley

Allow cheese to soften at room temperature. Crumble bleu cheese and grate sharp Cheddar cheese. You may use cheese bits in place of sharp cheese if desired. Mix together then add onion juice, pineapple juice and chopped pimento. Roll cheese mixture into balls and coat with parsley flakes. *Chill and serve. Makes 52 balls.*

CHEESE SAUCE

2 teaspoons flour
2 teaspoons butter, melted

½ cup milk
½ cup melted cheese

Combine ingredients and cook until smooth and thick.

STUFFED DEVILED EGGS

12 fresh eggs
1 small can potted meat
1 tablespoon chopped
   green pepper
1 small sweet pickle,
   chopped
¼ teaspoon pepper

1 teaspoon salt
¼ teaspoon onion juice
2 tablespoons mayonnaise
1 teaspoon prepared
   mustard
¼ teaspoon paprika

Place eggs in saucepan. Cover with cold water. Bring to a boil, turn down and simmer for 10 minutes. Cool immediately under cold water. Peel eggs. Cut in half lengthwise and remove yolks to a bowl. Set whites aside. Mix egg yolks with remaining ingredients except paprika. Stuff whites with mixture. Sprinkle with paprika. Serve immediately or refrigerate until serving time. *Serves 4 to 6.*

STUFFED CELERY

15 stalks celery
¾ cup pineapple-cream
   cheese spread

3 teaspoons pimento,
   chopped

Wash celery and cut into lengthwise pieces. Mix pineapple spread with pimento. Use mixture to fill cavity in celery pieces. Chill until ready to serve. *Serves 10-12.*

Good party snack.

GARLIC DIP

1 3-ounce package cream
  cheese, softened
2 ounces bleu cheese

1 cup sour cream
¼ cup garlic juice
½ cup crushed pineapple

Soften cheeses to room temperature. Blend all ingredients until smooth. Serve on Ritz crackers or with potato chips. *Good for a party!*

GRILLED CHEESE SANDWICH

2 tablespoons margarine
Mustard

2 slices white bread
2 slices American cheese

Melt margarine in skillet over medium high heat. Spread mustard on bread and put 2 slices cheese inside. Place sandwich in skillet and brown on both sides. Cut in half and serve immediately. *Serves 1.*

PEANUT BUTTER AND BANANA SANDWICH

3 tablespoons peanut
  butter
2 slices light bread

1 banana, mashed
2 tablespoons margarine,
  melted

Mix soft peanut butter and mashed banana together. Toast bread lightly. Spread peanut butter and mashed banana on toast. Place into melted margarine; brown on both sides.

PEANUT BUTTER SANDWICH

3 tablespoons peanut
    butter

4 slices bread
¼ cup margarine, melted

Toast bread lightly and spread with peanut butter. Place into medium hot margarine; brown on both sides. Serve immediately.

RED BRAID TWO PIECE SANDWICH

1 package franks
1 cup chili sauce
½ teaspoon mustard or
    mayonnaise

1 package buns
¼ teaspoon Tabasco sauce

Drop franks into boiling water. Cook until franks begin to expand. Warm buns in oven and split franks. Spoon chili sauce over franks. Add a drop of Tabasco sauce on each sandwich. *Makes 10 sandwiches.*

OPEN FACED SANDWICH

2 slices roast beef
1 or 2 slices toast

2 tablespoons brown gravy
Salt and pepper to taste

Put thinly sliced roast beef on toast and spoon hot gravy over it. Season with salt and pepper. Serve hot with mashed potatoes.

SPAM SANDWICH

1 can Spam, sliced
Mustard or salad dressing
Lettuce

Slices of tomato
Sliced dill pickles
Bread

Spread mustard or salad dressing on bread. Place Spam on bread and top with shredded lettuce, tomato slice, dill pickle. Serve with potato chips.

TOMATO SANDWICH

2 tomatoes, thinly sliced
2 slices white bread
½ teaspoon mayonnaise or
    mustard

2 thin slices of cheese
Salt and pepper to taste

Wash red ripe tomatoes and pat dry. Remove peel and slice. Lightly toast bread and spread with mustard or mayonnaise. Place tomatoes, cheese, and season to taste. Cut in half and serve.

STEWED SWEET TOMATOES

6 or 7 ripe tomatoes   **¼ cup butter or margarine**
3 cups water   **2 or 3 cooked biscuits**

Peel and cut tomatoes into pieces. Put into pot with 3 cups water and cook over medium heat; bring to boil. Add butter or margarine, sugar, and crumbled cold biscuits into tomatoes. Cook over low flame. *Serves 2 or 3.*

GRAPE JAM

3 pounds grapes   **5 cups sugar**
1 package Sure-Jell   **2 quarts water**

Wash grapes in cold water. Place into another kettle of water for cooking. Cook grapes until tender. Remove from heat. Cool. Mash grapes through cheesecloth so you get all juice and no seeds. Add sugar. Stir and add Sure-Jell. Place over medium heat; cook until bubbly. To test for doneness; drop a few drops into cold water; if it stands on top, it's ready. Let cool but do not chill. Pour into jars and seal.

CUCUMBER PICKLES

7 to 8 pounds cucumbers
Salt water
1 ½ quarts red vinegar
7 cups sugar

1 tablespoon celery seed
2 tablespoons allspice
1 teaspoon whole cloves
¼ teaspoon nutmeg

Soak cucumbers overnight in salt water. Rinse under cold water. In a pot bring vinegar to a boil and add the spices, which have been tied up in cheesecloth. Boil for 45 minutes. Remove from heat, put into jar, and leave space at the top. Seal tight.

WATERMELON RIND PICKLES

1 gallon peeled watermelon
   rinds
1 package pickling lime
5 pints white vinegar
6 cups sugar
½ ounce celery seed

1 teaspoon salt
1 ¾-ounce can stick
   cinnamon
1 tablespoon whole cloves
1 pint water

Peel all green from watermelon rind and cut into 1 inch chunks. Mix vinegar, sugar, celery seed and salt in large pot. Put cinnamon and cloves in cheesecloth and tie securely. Put spice bag in container with vinegar mixture and bring to a boil. Add watermelon rind and bring to boil again. Cook 1 hour or until rind is tender. Remove from heat and pack into hot, sterilized jars to ½ inch from top. Seal jars. *Makes 8 pints.*

Note: Good with peas.

FIG PRESERVES

3 quarts figs
2 pounds sugar
2 cups strawberries
1½ quart water

¼ teaspoon citric acid,
   optional
Sure-Jell

Wash figs and strawberries in cold water. Let fruit stand in sugar overnight; it will make its own syrup. Stir in water; then add Sure-Jell. Cook over medium heat until done. If desired use ¼ teaspoon citric acid so fruit won't turn dark. Seal into dry jars.

PICKLED PEACHES

9 pounds peaches
1 ounce cinnamon stick
2½ pounds sugar

1 quart red vinegar
1 ounce whole cloves
1 tablespoon allspice

Cook vinegar and all the spices together. Add sugar. Then add whole peaches into syrup. Let fruit cook until good and tender. Remove from heat. Cool before putting into jars. Use cheesecloth to hold spices if desired. Seal jars tight.

CHOW CHOW PICKLES

1 head green cabbage
1 dozen green tomatoes
1 or 2 red peppers
1 or 2 green peppers

4 cups sugar
1 quart red cider vinegar
1 teaspoon celery seed
3 tablespoons allspice

Use old hand grinder (or food processor) to grind cabbage, tomatoes, and peppers together. Mix sugar, vinegar and spices in saucepan. Bring to a boil and boil for 5 minutes. Add cabbage mixture and bring to a boil again. Cook about 3 to 5 minutes. Pour into pint jars and seal. Good with peas and greens.

Vernon loved this!

Breakfasts

BACON OMELET

4 eggs
1 tablespoon milk
Pinch salt
2 tablespoons Mazola
    margarine

¼ teaspoon pepper
½ cup bacon bits

Break eggs into a bowl and beat well. Add milk and pinch salt. Melt margarine in skillet and add eggs. Sprinkle pepper and bacon bits over eggs, fold and brown on both sides.

SCRAMBLED EGGS

5 eggs
1 tablespoon milk
Pinch salt

Pinch pepper
2 tablespoons butter

Break eggs into bowl and beat well. Add milk, salt, pepper. Melt butter in skillet and add eggs; stir. *Serve hot with biscuits and coffee.*

CANADIAN BACON BREAKFAST

6 slices Canadian bacon
Bacon grease
4 eggs

Salt and pepper
1 tablespoon milk
3 tablespoons butter

Fry Canadian bacon in bacon grease until light brown. Pat dry. Beat eggs, season to taste, and add milk. Melt butter in skillet, add eggs, and cook. *Serve with coffee and toast or crackers.*

EGG, ONION, AND PEPPER OMELET

5 eggs
1 tablespoon milk
¼ cup chopped onion
¹/₈ cup chopped green
  peppers

3 tablespoons Mazola
  margarine
Salt and pepper to taste

Mix eggs and milk together. Simmer onion and pepper in a little water until tender; drain. Melt margarine in skillet and add eggs. Fold in half and brown on both sides. *Serve hot.*

EGGS BENEDICT

3 poached eggs
2 English muffins
1 tomato, sliced

½ cup cheese sauce
3 slices bacon, ham, or
  sausage

Poach eggs over medium heat until soft. Toast English muffin; place eggs and tomato on muffin and cover with cheese sauce. Lay bacon, ham, or sausage around eggs, *Serve hot.*

EGG, HAM AND BACON OMELET

4 eggs
1 tablespoon milk
Salt and pepper to taste

¼ cup bacon bits
1 slice thin ham, chopped
3 tablespoons butter

Break eggs into bowl and beat. Add milk, salt, pepper, bacon bits, and pieces of ham. Heat butter in skillet and add egg mixture. Fold eggs in half and brown on both sides.

THIN HAM OMELET

5 eggs, well beaten
Salt and pepper to taste
1 tablespoon milk

3 tablespoons butter
2 slices thin chopped ham

Mix eggs, salt, pepper, and milk. Melt butter in skillet and add eggs. Add chopped ham; cook and fold over. Brown on both sides.

PORK BRAINS AND SCRAMBLED EGGS

1 pound brains
2 teaspoons vinegar
1 teaspoon seasoned salt

4 eggs, beaten
¼ cup bacon grease
Dash crushed red pepper

Wash brains in cold water, then put into one quart boiling water with 2 teaspoons vinegar and salt. Precook for 20 minutes. Drain and remove membrane, then season to taste. Add eggs. Heat bacon grease in skillet and pour in eggs and brain mixture. Stir together until done. If desired sprinkle crushed red pepper into brains while cooking.

FRENCH TOAST

2 eggs, well beaten
1 cup milk
4 slices white bread

2 teaspoons sugar and
   cinnamon
¼ cup Mazola margarine

Beat eggs; add milk, dip bread into batter. Sprinkle sugar and cinnamon on bread. Melt margarine in skillet and brown bread on both sides. *Serve immediately.*

CHEESE AND EGG OMELET

4 eggs
1 tablespoon milk
Pinch salt
1 teaspoon ground pepper

2 tablespoons butter or
    margarine
2 slices cheese, crumbled

Break eggs into bowl and beat. Add milk, pinch salt, and pepper. Melt butter in skillet and add eggs; let cook. Crumble cheese on eggs and fold egg mixture over. Cook until brown on both sides. *Serve immediately.*

GRANDMA'S BREAKFAST

2 slices bacon
1 slice country ham
½ cup strong black coffee
2 eggs

2 hot biscuits
Butter
Syrup
2 cups coffee with cream

Cook bacon until crisp. Remove from skillet and add ham. Fry ham until lightly browned. Pour off all grease leaving about 3 tablespoons in skillet. Pour ½ cup coffee over ham in skillet and simmer for 3 or 4 minutes. Remove to plate, pouring red-eye gravy on top of ham. *Serve with eggs, hot biscuits, syrup and butter.*

OLD FASHIONED SUGAR SYRUP

1 cup sugar
3 tablespoons butter

¾ cup water
1 teaspoon vanilla

Pour water into skillet. Add sugar, butter and vanilla and stir and heat. When it starts getting thick, remove from heat. *Serve with hot country biscuits.*

PIG IN THE SANDWICH

6 Tennessee Pride sausages   6 homemade biscuits

Fry sausages then place into biscuits. Warm in oven 3 to 5 minutes. *Serve with grape jelly and Mazola margarine.*

CREAMED WHEAT

3 cups water or milk
½ teaspoon salt

2 tablespoons Mazola margarine
1 cup creamed wheat

Put water into kettle and let it boil. Add salt and margarine; stir in creamed wheat. Add milk to keep from becoming stiff. Cook 15 to 20 minutes. *Serve with butter.*

"COUNT YOUR CALORIES"
DIET SUBSTITUTE BREAKFAST

1 slice Canadian bacon, 57 calories
1 slice toast, 25 calories
1 boiled egg, 75 calories
1 bowl corn flakes, 80 calories
Black coffee

1 8-ounce glass orange juice, 115 calories
1 poached egg, 75 calories
1 slice whole wheat toast, 55 calories

100 Percent Bran Flakes, 195 calories
2 slices bacon, 98 calories
½ grapefruit, 60 calories
Coffee with cream, 4 calories

This is what I ate when I was on my diet. I counted my calories and lost 50 pounds in 3 months.

VESTER'S DIET

Breakfast:

1 slice dry toast
½ grapefruit
1 box Egg Beaters

1 slice bacon
Orange juice or black coffee

Dinner:

Fresh fruit
1 can cut green beans

4 ounces lean meat
1 8-ounce glass buttermilk

Cook all vegetables with Mazola margarine. Vester lost 17 pounds on this diet.

Breads

SWIRL MONKEY BREAD

4½ cups flour
½ cup sugar
½ teaspoon salt
2 ounces shortening
3 tablespoons butter or
    margarine

2 eggs, beaten
1 cup Irish potato water
2 envelopes yeast
¾ cup warm water
¼ cup sesame seeds

Sift flour and sugar into a large bowl and add ½ teaspoon salt. Mix shortening and butter or margarine together into flour mixture. Add beaten eggs. Dissolve yeast in warm water and add to mixture, along with Irish potato water. Knead dough thoroughly and add flour as needed to make dough easy to handle. Turn dough into a greased bowl and let stand in a warm place until it has risen. Punch dough down and let it rise again. Roll dough into a ½-inch thick sheet and cut out several rectangular oblongs. Twist dough and pull to elongate. Dip each roll into melted butter and place rolls side by side in a greased pan. Sprinkle seeds on top of dough and let rise once more. Bake at 400 degrees for ½ hour, then at 375 degrees for a second ½ hour.

CINNAMON BREAD LOAF

4½ cups sifted flour
Pinch of salt
¼ cup sugar
1 package dry yeast
1¼ cups milk

2 eggs, beaten
½ cup butter
2 teaspoons cinnamon
Sesame seed

Sift flour, pinch of salt, and sugar. Dissolve yeast in milk and pour into flour. Add beaten eggs, melted butter, and cinnamon. Add enough flour to make dough easy to handle, knead, and place in greased bowl. Let dough stand for 30 minutes in a warm place and allow to rise. Punch down, knead again and let dough rise again. Punch down, roll in melted butter, and place in a greased loaf pan. Sprinkle sesame seeds over the top. Bake at 350 degrees for 45 minutes.

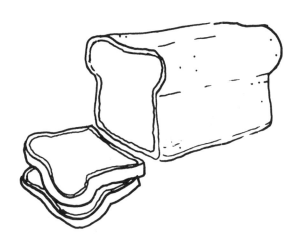

BLUEBERRY MUFFINS

1½ cups plain flour
1 teaspoon baking powder
½ teaspoon salt
½ cup sugar
¼ cup Crisco oil

½ cup milk
1 egg
1 small can blueberries, drained

Mix in a large bowl: flour, baking powder, salt and sugar. Then add oil, milk, and egg. Stir in blueberries. Beat batter until smooth. Pour into greased muffin pan and bake for 25 minutes at 350 degrees. *Yield: 12 muffins.*

HOME MADE BISCUITS

3 cups self-rising flour,
   sifted
1 teaspoon baking powder

¼ teaspoon sugar
½ cup Crisco shortening
¾ cup buttermilk

Preheat oven to 375 degrees. In a large bowl mix flour, baking powder, and sugar. Work Crisco into flour until it is the consistency of course meal. Add milk. Knead dough thoroughly, adding flour to make dough easy to handle. Sprinkle flour on cutting board and roll dough out to ½ inch, cut biscuits out and place in shallow pan to bake. Cook 15 to 20 minutes.

EASY BROWN HOT ROLLS

1 package dry yeast
2 cups warm water
4 cups self-rising flour
Dash salt

½ cup sugar
1 teaspoon baking powder
¾ cup butter
2 eggs

Dissolve yeast in warm water. Combine flour, dash salt, sugar, and baking powder. Beat. Add butter and eggs. Add enough flour so dough will be easy to handle, and thoroughly knead the dough. Place dough in a greased bowl and allow dough to rise. Punch it down, and it is ready to cook. You may spoon batter into greased muffin pans or cut rolls out. Bake at 375 degrees for 15 to 20 minutes.

OLD FASHIONED BUTTER ROLL

1 quart milk
2½ cups sugar
1 teaspoon vanilla
3 or 4 cups flour

Pinch salt
½ cup butter
1 grated orange rind

Pour milk into a bowl. Sweeten to own taste. Add vanilla to milk. Stir in flour in make a dough. Roll dough ½-inch thick. Cut into large pieces; fold part sugar, butter, grated orange rind into each piece of dough and fold over. Place in pan and sprinkle sugar over top of dough. Dot with butter. Bake in 375 degree oven for 25 minutes.

SOUTHERN CRACKLING BREAD

1 pound cracklings
½ teaspoon salt
1 teaspoon baking powder

1 egg, beaten
2½ cups yellow corn meal
¾ cup hot water

Let cracklings soak overnight in 1 cup of warm water. Mix salt, baking powder, and yellow corn meal, and beat egg into this mixture. Add ¾ cup hot water. Beat batter and pour into skillet or pan. Bake at 400 degrees until brown, about 20 to 30 minutes.

CORN BREAD

3 cups self-rising corn
   meal
2 tablespoons self-rising
   flour
1 teaspoon baking powder

1 teaspoon sugar
1¼ cups milk
2 eggs
1 tablespoon butter
2 tablespoons Crisco

Sift corn meal and flour together. Add baking powder, sugar, milk, and beat smooth. Add eggs, melted butter and Crisco. Stir. Pour into greased pan that has been sprinkled with corn meal. Bake 20 to 25 minutes at 425 to 450 degrees.

PIZZA CRUST

1 package dry yeast
1 cup warm water
2½ cups self-rising flour

3 tablespoons Crisco
Pinch salt
1 teaspoon sugar

Dissolve yeast in warm water. Stir in flour, Crisco, salt and sugar. Work dough until easy to handle. Cover bowl and let rise for 5 minutes. Roll out and shape in pizza pan. Use sauce and cheese as desired.

HOME MADE PANCAKES

1½ cups self-rising flour
2 tablespoons sugar
½ teaspoon cinnamon
⅔ cup milk

1 egg
3 tablespoons butter,
   melted
Butter for skillet

In a large bowl mix flour, sugar, cinnamon, milk, and egg. Pour melted butter into batter and beat until smooth. Melt extra butter in skillet and add batter by large spoonfuls. Brown on both sides. *Yield: 4 pancakes.*

Salads and Soups

AMBROSIA

5 medium oranges, peeled
   and sectioned
2 cups white seedless
   grapes
1 16-ounce bottle ginger
   ale
1 8-ounce jar maraschino
   cherries

3 large bananas, diced
1 3½-ounce can moist
   coconut
1 16-ounce can pineapple
   chunks, drained
1 cup Sun-Maid raisins

Mix all ingredients and chill until ready to serve.

AMBROSIA SALAD

2 cups purple grapes
1 can pineapple chunks,
   drained
4 tangerines, peeled and
   sectioned
1 3½-ounce can moist
   coconut
2 bananas, sliced

1 small jar cherries,
   drained
1 grapefruit, peeled and
   sectioned
1 large orange, peeled and
   sectioned
3 tablespoons salad
   dressing

Mix ingredients together; add salad dressing. Stir and chill until
ready to serve.

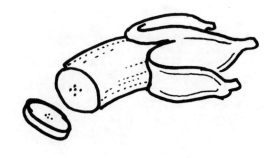

WALDORF SALAD

1 cup white raisins
1 carrot, grated
½ pound white seedless
    grapes
1 banana, sliced

1 cup apple, diced
⅓ cup almonds, sliced
1 cup pineapple, diced
2 tablespoons mayonnaise

Toss fruit and almonds together and stir in mayonnaise. Chill.
Serve on lettuce.

BAKED APPLES

6 apples
½ cup sugar
3 teaspoons cinnamon
Lemon juice

½ cup brown sugar
½ cup butter
1 teaspoon apple pie spice

Wash and core the apples. Cover the bottom of a pan with a little
water. Put apples into pan; add sugars and spices. Put some butter
in the apples. Add a few drops of lemon juice, if desired, to keep
apples from turning dark. Bake in a 350 degree oven for about 30
to 45 minutes.

OLD FASHIONED FRIED APPLES

6 apples
1 teaspoon apple pie spice
2 teaspoons sugar and
   cinnamon
1 cup flour

Pinch salt
1 teaspoon baking powder
2 tablespoons Crisco oil
1/2 cup water

Peel and slice apples into quarters. Sprinkle apple pie spice, sugar and cinnamon on apples. Make a batter of flour, salt, baking powder, oil and water. Make batter stiff enough so you can roll apples over and over into batter. Then drop apples into hot oil; fry until tender and brown.

BAKED BANANAS

6 bananas
3 tablespoons brown sugar
1/4 cup margarine

1 1/2 tablespoons lemon
   juice

Remove banana peel and split lengthwise. Place in pan with brown sugar and melted margarine. Pour lemon juice over bananas. Bake in 375 degree oven for 3-5 minutes until golden brown.

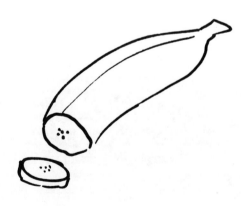

COTTAGE CHEESE AND PEACHES

2 cups cottage
   cheese

1 16-ounce can sliced
   peaches

Layer peaches and cottage cheese in bowl. Chill and serve. *This is a good diet meal.*

PEAR SALAD

1 package lime Jello
1 cup water
1 15½-ounce can pears,
   drained
½ cup white raisins
1 small can white grapes

¼ cup pineapple chunks,
   drained
1 3-ounce package cream
   cheese, softened
1 tablespoon salad
   dressing

Dissolve Jello in 1 cup hot water, and let it partially congeal. Drain pears and cut into pieces. Combine raisins, grapes, pineapple, and softened cream cheese. Add fruits to soft set Jello along with the salad dressing. Stir to blend. Serve on lettuce leaf. Keep in refrigerator until ready to serve. *Serves 4 or 5.*

COTTAGE CHEESE STRAWBERRY MOLD

1 3-ounce package
strawberry flavored
gelatin

1 cup cottage cheese
1 small Cool Whip

Mix gelatin according to package directions. Divide gelatin into 3 parts. Chill one part; mix cottage cheese with one part and pour onto plain layer and pour one part on top. Chill each part before adding another. Congeal firmly. top with Cool Whip. Keep in refrigerator until ready to serve.

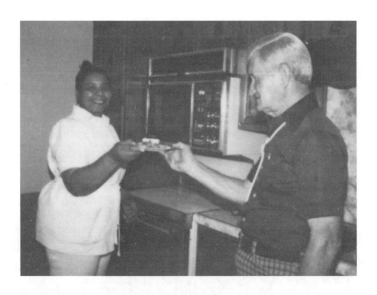

FRESH PINEAPPLE STUFFED WITH FRUIT

1 fresh pineapple
1 cup coconut flakes
1 cup watermelon balls
1 ½ cups honeydew balls
1 cup white grapes
1 pear, sliced
1 cup cottage cheese

1 tangerine, peeled and
  sectioned
1 cup pitted prunes
1 cup cantaloupe balls
1 pint fresh strawberries
1 apple diced

Cut pineapple in half lengthwise. Remove pineapple fruit leaving the outer shell intact. Cut pineapple fruit into chunks. Mix with other fruit, coconut, and cottage cheese. Fill both halves of pineapple shell. Chill until ready to serve. *Good for holidays or buffet dinners.*

FRUIT SALAD FOR THE HOLIDAYS

5 Delicious apples
3 large oranges
2 tangerines
½ cup white raisins
⅓ cup red cherries

3 bananas
½ cup miniature
  marshmallows
2 tablespoons mayonnaise

Peel apples, then dice into small pieces. Pare and section oranges and tangerines. Mix cherries, raisins, apples, oranges, and tangerines with mayonnaise. Chill. Just before serving stir in bananas and marshmallows. Garnish with a few more cherries. *Serves 8 or 9.*

LARGE MIXED FRUIT SALAD

2 cups apples	2 cups pears
2 cups grapefruit sections	2 cups orange sections
2 cups peaches	¼ cup salad dressing
1 cup seedless white grapes	1 cup cherries
1 medium nectarine	2 cups cottage cheese
1 cup white raisins	1 cup fresh strawberries

Wash and peel fresh. Dice or slice into small pieces. If canned fruit is used, drain well. Mix fruit and salad dressing together. Drain cottage cheese; pour over top of fruits. Top with a few strawberries or cherries. Chill for 1 hour. Serve on lettuce leaves.

COLA SALAD

1 large package black cherry Jello	½ cup chopped pecans
	½ cup white grapes
1 15-ounce can crushed pineapple, drained	1 8-ounce package cream cheese, softened
1 cup apple, chopped	1 king size cola soft drink
1 cup white seedless raisins	

Mix Jello according to package directions. Add remaining ingredients except cola and mix well. Add cola last and stir. Pour into lightly oiled salad mold. Refrigerate at least 6 hours before serving. *Serves 6-8.*

COMBINATION SALAD

½ head chopped lettuce
5 radishes, thinly sliced
½ cup chopped onions
1 large diced tomato

2 medium-sized cucumbers, sliced
Pinch salt

Combine all ingredients. Toss high; serve with your choice of dressing.

APPETIZER GREEN SALAD

1 head Romaine lettuce
½ cup black olives
2 large banana peppers
½ cup chopped green onions
1 small can sliced mushrooms

12 cherry tomatoes
½ cup green olives
2 cucumbers, sliced
6 pickled okra pods
¼ cup finely chopped celery
5 large radishes
½ cup red wine vinegar

Chop all ingredients. Mix in a large bowl and chill. Serve with red wine vinegar or bleu cheese dressing. *6 or 7 servings.*

FALL COLE SLAW

1 cup ham, chopped
1 head cabbage, grated
2 small cucumbers, sliced
  thin
1 green pepper, chopped
1 onion, chopped
1 large green tomato,
  chopped

3 large radishes, sliced thin
1 tablespoon sugar
2 tablespoons red vinegar
1 teaspoon prepared
  mustard
2 tablespoons mayonnaise
Salt and pepper

Combine all ingredients. Stir and chill well before serving. *Serves 4-6.*

GREEN COLE SLAW

1 small cabbage, grated
2 teaspoons vinegar
2 teaspoons sugar
2 tablespoons mayonnaise

1 banana pepper or bell
  pepper, chopped
1 small onion, grated

Combine all ingredients in a small bowl and serve. *Good on fish or hot dogs.*

CHEESE SALAD

1 cup cubed Cheddar
   cheese
3 - 4 slices American cheese
2 small cucumbers, sliced
4 large radishes, sliced
1 cup salami, chopped
2 cups bologna, chopped

4 hard boiled eggs,
   chopped
½ cup bacon bits
1 2½-ounce can sliced
   mushrooms
1 small head lettuce

Cut or tear lettuce into pieces as for salad. Mix with remaining ingredients, omitting sliced American cheese. Place in salad bowl and top with American cheese cut in half to form triangles. Serve with dressing of your choice.

Note: Good with Green Onion Dressing or vinegar and oil!

AUTUMN KIDNEY BEAN SALAD

1 16-ounce can kidney
   beans
¼ cup chopped celery
⅓ cup chopped onion
¼ cup chopped sweet pickle
3 hard boiled eggs,
   chopped

1 tablespoon salad
   dressing
2 teaspoons prepared
   mustard
½ teaspoon sugar
Salt and pepper

Simmer kidney beans over medium heat for 5 minutes. Cool. Add remaining ingredients and mix well. Chill until ready to serve. *Serves 4-6.*

Note: If desired, add ¼ cup chopped green pepper.

ENGLISH PEA SALAD

1 16-ounce can English peas	1 1½-ounce jar pimento
1 bunch green onions	½ cup bacon bits
½ cup chopped celery	1 cup sour cream
¼ cup chopped green pepper	2 tablespoons red vinegar
1 cup chopped cooked ham	3 hard-boiled eggs
	1 tablespoon sugar
	Salt and pepper to taste

Drain English peas; pour into bowl. Add chopped green onions, celery, green pepper, cooked ham, chopped pimento and bacon bits. Stir in sour cream, red vinegar, chopped boiled eggs and sugar. Season with salt and pepper to own taste. Mix well and chill until ready to serve.

BOLOGNA SALAD

3 cups bologna	2 hard-boiled eggs, chopped
½ cup celery, chopped	1 cup potato chips, crushed
¼ cup onions, minced	2 teaspoons mustard
2 teaspoons pepper	1 tablespoon salad dressing
⅓ cup sweet pickles, diced	
¼ cup croutons	

Chop or dice bologna. Add finely chopped celery, minced onion, pepper, sweet pickles, croutons, and boiled eggs. Add potato chips, mustard, and salad dressing; mix well; chill. Serve on lettuce.

CHICKEN SALAD

8 cups cooked chicken,
   diced
¼ cup chopped sweet pickle
1 teaspoon mustard
1 tablespoon sugar
¼ cup chopped celery

¼ cup chopped bell pepper
   (optional)
⅓ cup chopped onion
4 hard-boiled eggs,
   chopped
2 tablespoons mayonnaise

Mix above ingredients together and put in large bowl. Sprinkle with paprika and refrigerate until ready to serve. *Serves 6.*

EGG SALAD

½ cup finely chopped celery
2 tablespoons minced
   onion
¼ cup chopped sweet
   pickles

1 teaspoon paprika
½ dozen eggs
½ teaspoon dry mustard
1 tablespoon salad
   dressing

Boil eggs; chop or dice them. Mix other ingredients into eggs; mix well. Serve warm or cold.

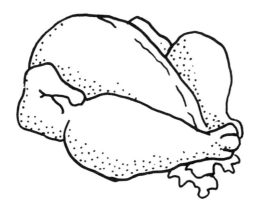

HAM SALAD

3 cups chopped or deviled
  ham
1/3 cup chopped onion
Salt and pepper to taste
1 teaspoon mustard

2/3 cup chopped celery
1/4 cup chopped sweet pickle
3 hard-boiled eggs
2 tablespoons salad
  dressing

Mix all ingredients together. Serve with dill pickle and/or tomatoes on the side.

ELBOW MACARONI SALAD

1 5-ounce package elbow
  macaroni
Salt and pepper
1/3 cup chopped onion
1/4 cup chopped green
  pepper

1/4 cup chopped celery
1 chopped sweet pickle
4 hard-boiled eggs
1 tablespoon mayonnaise
2 teaspoons mustard

Cook macaroni in boiling salted water until tender. Do not over-cook. Drain macaroni and salt and pepper to taste. Mix onion, green pepper, celery, sweet pickle, and 3 chopped hard-boiled eggs into macaroni. Reserve 1 hard-boiled egg for topping. If desired, sprinkle a little sugar or sweet pickle juice into mixture. Add mayonnaise and mustard and mix well. Slice 1 hard-boiled egg over the top of salad and sprinkle a little paprika on it. *Serves 5 or more.*

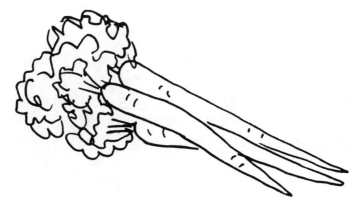

GERMAN POTATO SALAD

5 or 6 cups cooked
  potatoes
Salt and pepper
1 teaspoon dry mustard
1 teaspoon parsley flakes
2 tablespoons melted
  butter
1 small jar artichokes in oil

½ cup chopped onion
½ cup chopped celery
½ cup chopped green
  pepper
¼ cup chopped sweet
  pickles
5 hard-boiled eggs
½ cup salad dressing

Wash, peel and dice potatoes. Cook in cold water until tender and drain. Add salt and pepper to taste, dry mustard, parsley flakes, butter, finely chopped artichokes and oil. Simmer onion, celery, and green pepper in butter for 5 minutes. Stir into salad with sweet pickles and sliced boiled eggs. Stir in salad dressing. Serve hot or warm.

POTATO SALAD

4 medium potatoes
½ teaspoon salt
1 teaspoon pepper
⅓ cup finely chopped onion
¼ cup chopped green
  pepper
¼ cup chopped celery
⅓ sweet pickle, chopped
4 hard-boiled eggs,
  chopped

2 tablespoons sweet pickle
  juice
1 tablespoon parsley flakes
3 tablespoons salad
  dressing
1 teaspoon prepared
  mustard
6 stuffed olives, sliced
½ teaspoon paprika

Cook potatoes and drain. Let potatoes cool, then dice. Add salt and pepper, chopped onions, bell pepper, celery, sweet pickles, boiled eggs, and pickle juice. Mix well with rest of ingredients. Sprinkle paprika over top. Serve warm or cold.

POTATO SALAD

2 large potatoes
1 cup finely chopped celery
½ cup chopped sweet onion
¼ cup chopped sweet pickle
3 hard-boiled eggs,
  chopped

¼ teaspoon nutmeg
⅔ cup salad dressing
1 teaspoon vinegar
1 teaspoon black pepper
½ teaspoon salt

Wash potatoes, peel and dice. Cook until tender. Drain. Add remaining ingredients and mix well. Chill. *Serves 4-6.*

SHRIMP SALAD

1 to 2 pounds fresh shrimp
4 cups cooked fluffy rice
¼ cup chopped celery
¼ cup chopped green
  pepper
¼ cup chopped onion
3 hard-boiled eggs

½ teaspoon Morton's
  seasoned salt
1 teaspoon dry mustard
1 teaspoon dill seed
1 teaspoon pepper
⅓ cup chopped pimento
Paprika

Boil shrimp, cool and peel. Chop if desired. Mix all ingredients well except boiled eggs and paprika. Place salad in bowl and top with sliced boiled eggs and paprika. Chill 3 to 4 hours. *Serves 5-6.*

TUNA SALAD

2 8½-ounce cans tuna
¼ cup chopped celery
½ cup chopped onion
¼ cup chopped sweet pickle
2 hard-boiled eggs,
    chopped

1 teaspoon mustard
2 tablespoons mayonnaise
½ teaspoon salt
Dash pepper

Mix first five ingredients in large bowl. Add mayonnaise and mustard, salt and pepper. Stir well. Place in salad bowl and sprinkle with paprika. Sliced boiled egg may also be used as garnish. Chill well before serving. *Serves 6-8.*

This salad may be served heated on toast.

RICE SALAD

2 cups fluffy cooked long-
    grained rice
4 hard-boiled eggs
¼ cup chopped celery
⅓ cup chopped onion
1 cup sliced mushrooms
⅓ cup chopped green
    pepper

1 teaspoon salt
1 teaspoon lemon-pepper
1 tablespoon salad
    dressing
2 teaspoons mustard
1 package smoked turkey
    or salami, cut up

Mix all ingredients together, reserving 1 egg. Place in salad bowl and top with 1 boiled egg, sliced and sprinkled with paprika. *Serves 6.*

COLD TURKEY SALAD

4 cups cooked turkey
1 teaspoon pepper
½ teaspoon salt
½ cup chopped onion
½ cup chopped celery
¼ cup chopped sweet pickle

4 hard-boiled eggs
¼ cup chopped mushrooms
½ teaspoon mustard
3 tablespoons salad
  dressing
¼ teaspoon paprika

This is a good way to use leftover turkey from Thanksgiving. Remove any skin from meat and cut the white meat and dark meat together. Place meat in a large bowl, then add salt, pepper, onions, celery, sweet pickle, hard-boiled eggs, and chopped mushrooms. Stir together, then mix in mustard and salad dressing. Place in a glass dish; sprinkle paprika over the top. Chill before serving. *Serves 5 or 6.*

POTATO SOUP

5 or 6 medium potatoes
2½ cups milk
½ teaspoon salt
½ teaspoon pepper

3 tablespoons butter
1 teaspoon parsley flakes
¹/₈ cup onion juice
1 tablespoon flour

Peel potatoes, rinse them off, and cut them into quarter pieces. Place in pot with milk, salt, pepper, butter, parsley, and onion juice. Let potatoes cook until they are almost done. Add flour in a little water to pot and stir until smooth. Pour milk into potato mixture, mash the potatoes and stir until smooth. Serve with crackers.

HOMEMADE TOMATO SOUP

2 16-ounce cans whole
   tomatoes
½ teaspoon salt

1 teaspoon pepper
¼ cup bacon grease
1 cup corn meal

Cook whole tomatoes until they fall apart. Strain off juice. Add salt, pepper and bacon grease to tomato juice; stir in corn meal. Cook clowly until smooth and thick. Serve with hot corn bread. *Serves 4.*

Note: My mother used to make this soup long years ago for us when we were children. This is the last thing she made before she completely stopped cooking. She made this soup about 6 years ago, with a little help from my daughter and one of the maids, because she was not able to stand up for long periods of time. She was a very good cook. There is one cook almost as good as my mother. She is the one who helped me prepare this cookbook.

QUICK MIXTURE-VEGETABLE SOUP

1 10¾-ounce can tomato
   soup
1 10¾-ounce can chicken
   noodle soup
2 teaspoons black pepper
2 tablespoons bacon
   grease

1 10¾-ounce can old-
   fashioned vegetable
   soup
2 cans cold water
1 4-ounce can mushroom
   soup
1 can potato soup

Mix all soups together in a large kettle. Add 1 can of water for each can of soup. Stir and season with pepper. Add bacon grease, cook for 20 minutes. Serve hot with crackers. *Serves 3 or 4.*

Poultry, Game and Fish

SMOTHERED CHICKEN

1 whole chicken, cut into
    pieces
2 teaspoons salt
1½ teaspoons ground
    pepper

1 cup flour
1 small onion, sliced
¼ cup butter
1 cup water

Cut chicken into large pieces. Add salt and pepper; sprinkle on chicken. Roll over in 1 cup flour or shake in a paper bag with flour. Place chicken into skillet in 1 cup water and butter. Slice onion over chicken pieces. Cover skillet with lid. Put into oven and bake at 400 degrees for 30 minutes. Remove lid and let chicken brown toward the end.

CHICKEN À LA KING

¼ cup chopped onion
¼ cup chopped green
    pepper
⅓ cup chopped mushrooms
½ cup margarine
1 cup chicken broth
½ teaspoon salt

¼ teaspoon pepper
⅛ teaspoon garlic powder
⅓ cup sour cream
3 cups cubed, cooked
    chicken
1 small jar pimento
Paprika

Simmer green pepper, mushrooms and onion in margarine until tender. Add broth with salt, pepper, and garlic powder. Stir in sour cream, cubes of chicken and pimento. Simmer for 15 to 20 minutes. Sprinkle with paprika. Serve over toast.

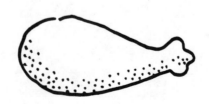

CHICKEN AND NOODLES

1 whole chicken, cut up	1/3 cup chopped celery
1 package Ronco egg noodles	1 teaspoon basil leaves
1 teaspoon parsley flakes	1 15-ounce can whole tomatoes
1/4 cup butter	1/2 teaspoon garlic powder
1/2 cup minced onion	Salt and pepper to taste

Place cut-up chicken in enough water to cover it and cook until the meat pulls away from the bone. Remove bones and tear chicken meat into pieces. Cook noodles and drain. Add chicken and noodles to broth. Mix in remainder of ingredients and simmer for 45 minutes to 1 hour until thick. *Serves 8.*

SOUTHERN FRIED CHICKEN

1 whole fryer	2 teaspoons salt
1 1/2 cups flour	1/2 bottle Crisco oil
1 teaspoon pepper	Sprinkle paprika

Cut chicken into pieces; wash, then pat dry. Shake chicken and seasonings and flour together in paper bag. Put into hot Crisco oil; brown. To make crispy fried chicken: beat 2 eggs and 1 cup of milk together. Dip pieces of chicken into batter, then roll over in flour and cook until golden brown.

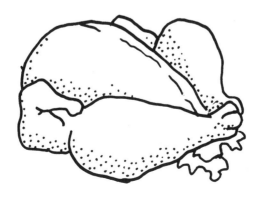

ROOK'S CHICKEN AND SPAGHETTI

Chicken:

1 3 to 4-pound hen, cut up   1 teaspoon salt
1 quart water

Cook chicken in saucepan with water and salt until tender. Remove from broth and cool enough to handle. Skin and remove bones from chicken pieces. Set meat aside while making sauce.

Spaghetti sauce:

½ cup chopped bell pepper   2 4-ounce cans sliced
½ cup chopped onion   mushrooms, drained
⅓ cup chopped celery   1 package dry spaghetti
¼ cup margarine   sauce mix
2 8-ounce cans tomato   Salt and pepper to taste
    sauce

Sauté bell pepper, onion, and celery in margarine until tender but not brown. Add tomato sauce, mushrooms and dry spaghetti mix. Season with salt and pepper to taste. Simmer while cooking spaghetti.

Spaghetti:

1 8-ounce package   2 quarts water
    spaghetti

Cook spaghetti in boiling water as directed on package. Drain.

Preheat oven to 350 degrees. To assemble casserole, stir spaghetti, chicken, and sauce together. Pour into a buttered casserole dish. Top with cheese slices. Bake at 350 degrees for 15 minutes or until cheese is melted. *Serves 4 to 6.*

COUNTRY FRIED CHICKEN

1 whole chicken, cut up	1 ½ cups plain flour
1 teaspoon ground pepper	2 cups shortening
1 teaspoon salt	

Wash chicken and pat dry; cut into pieces. Season chicken with salt and pepper. Put flour and chicken pieces into paper bag. Shake to coat chicken. Drop chicken pieces into skillet of hot oil. Fry until golden brown.

BREADED CHICKEN LIVERS

1 pound chicken livers	¼ cup minced onion
1 teaspoon seasoned salt	Pinch curry powder
1 teaspoon ground pepper	1 cup Crisco oil
1 cup flour	

Wash chicken livers in cold water. Pat dry. Sprinkle with salt and pepper. Combine flour, minced onion and curry powder. Coat chicken livers in flour mixture. Fry in hot oil in skillet until done.

BREADED CHICKEN GIZZARDS

1 pound chicken gizzards
1 cup plain flour
2 teaspoons seasoned salt
2 teaspoons pepper

1 egg
3 tablespoons milk
1 cup Crisco oil
Pinch paprika

Wash chicken gizzards in cold water, put into salted boiling water and cook until tender. Drain. Beat egg and milk together. Stir gizzards in. Mix flour, salt and pepper then coat chicken gizzards; sprinkle with paprika. Drop in hot oil and cook until lightly browned. Remove from oil and serve immediately.

WILD RICE AND GIZZARDS

1 pound chicken gizzards
½ cup Mazola margarine
1 teaspoon seasoned salt
1 teaspoon lemon pepper
3½ cups long grain wild
   rice

¼ teaspoon curry powder
½ cup sliced mushrooms
⅓ cup chopped onion
1 tablespoon chopped
   green pepper

Wash gizzards, put into cold water and cook with margarine, seasoned salt, and pepper until almost done. Pour rice into pot, stir, and add curry powder, mushroom, chopped onion, and green pepper. Let rice and gizzards cook over a very low flame and serve hot. *Serves 3 or 4.*

OLD FASHIONED BARBECUED CHICKEN

1 whole chicken
½ cup water
½ cup catsup
½ cup margarine, melted
2 teaspoons smoke salt

½ teaspoon pepper
2 tablespoons vinegar
⅓ cup molasses
1 teaspoon dry mustard
¼ teaspoon hot sauce

Cut chicken up into pieces; arrange in dish. Mix water, melted margarine and catsup together; stir in seasonings and vinegar. Brush mixture over chicken pieces. Cook uncovered for 30 minutes at 350 degrees. Mix molasses, dry mustard and hot sauce and spoon over chicken pieces. Cook 20-25 minutes more.

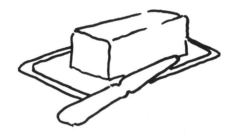

BAKED HEN AND DRESSING

1 5-pound hen
1 teaspoon pepper
3 eggs, beaten
¼ cup chopped green
    pepper
1 tablespoon sugar
10 cups corn bread crumbs
    or 1 package corn bread
    stuffing

1 teaspoon salt
3 teaspoons sage
½ cup chopped onion
¼ teaspoon garlic powder
1 can cream of celery soup
8 cups chicken broth
3 quarts cold water
¼ cup white raisins

Wash hen. Put hen in cold water. While hen is cooking, add a few chopped onions, celery, salt, and pepper into the broth. When hen gets tender enough to stick a fork into; remove from broth. Cook cornbread; add a little chopped onion into batter. After bread is done; cool it and add salt, pepper, chopped onion, garlic, bell-pepper, sage, sugar, white raisins, soup and eggs. Baste hen with butter; put into pan and bake in oven until brown, at 350 degrees for 1 hour. Cook stuffing slowly for 25 to 30 minutes until brown. Serve with baked hen and cranberry sauce.

CHICKEN GUMBO

1 chicken
1 teaspoon salt
1 teaspoon curry powder
1 teaspoon lemon pepper
1/3 cup chopped green
   pepper
1/2 cup plain flour
1 package frozen cut okra

1 1/2 cups Riceland rice
1/2 cup Mazola margarine
1/2 cup chopped onion
1 15 1/2-ounce can whole
   kernel corn
1 15 1/2-pounce can whole
   tomatoes

Cook chicken in water until tender. Remove chicken from broth. Cook rice in chicken broth. Cut chicken into parts. Roll over in flour, curry powder, salt and pepper; lightly brown chicken. Pour rice into casserole dish. Add chicken, green pepper, onion, cut okra, corn, margarine, and whole tomatoes. Place into oven; cover dish. Cook for 1 hour at 325 degrees.

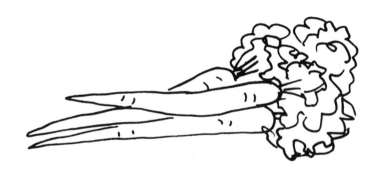

CHICKEN BRUNSWICK STEW

1 large chicken
1 box frozen cut okra
1 large can tomato sauce
1 large onion, chopped
1 can cream style corn
6 medium potatoes, diced

2 cans whole kernel corn
2 cans whole peeled
   tomatoes
1/2 pound bacon, diced
1/2 cup celery, diced
1/4 cup chopped bell pepper

Cover chicken with water and cook until meat falls off the bone. Remove bones and cut chicken into pieces. Add vegetables, tomato sauce and chopped bacon into chicken broth. Cook for 1 hour over low heat or until mixture is thick. *Serves 10.*

NECK BONES WITH DRESSING

2 pounds neck bones
1 cup chopped celery
1 garlic clove, crushed
2 eggs
Pinch sugar
4 or 5 cups broth
1 cup chopped onion

1 teaspoon poultry
  seasoning
1 tablespoon sage
Salt and pepper to taste
¼ cup sherry wine
1 package stuffing mix

Boil neck bones in water for 5 minutes; pour water off and put them into more fresh water. Cook with salt and pepper. Drop a few pieces of celery and onion into the pot with neck bones while they are cooking to flavor the broth. After neck bones are done, remove from broth. Strain. In a little oil, simmer celery, onion, garlic until tender, then pour into stuffing with dry seasoning and beaten egg. Pour in broth gradually and stir. Add sherry wine last. Stir. Now you are ready to bake in oven at 375 degrees until brown about 40 minutes. Spread neckbones around stuffing and serve.

TURKEY AND DRESSING

12 pound turkey
¼ cup bell pepper, chopped
1 teaspoon salt
3 eggs, beaten
½ cup seedless white
    raisins

1 cup onion, chopped
½ cup chopped celery
2 teaspoons ground pepper
¼ cup sage
8 cups bread crumbs

Cook turkey in oven; baste with butter and wrap in foil. Use turkey parts for stuffing. Boil turkey parts in water with celery, onions, salt, and pepper until done. Cook corn bread; add some onion in bread. Simmer other ingredients, chopped bell pepper, onion and celery in a little cooking oil until tender. Pour into bread crumbs. Mix white raisins into crumbs. Pour broth gradually into crumbs. Pour into pan and bake at 475 degrees for 45 minutes.

BOILED-FRIED QUAIL

6 quail
3½ cups water
1 teaspoon salt

1 teaspoon pepper
1 cup flour
½ cup Crisco oil

Parboil quail until tender; drain. Season and coat in flour. Place into hot oil and brown. *Serves 2.*

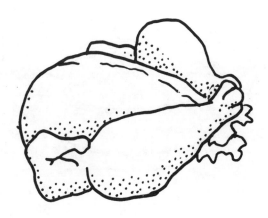

DUCK DRESSING

5 pound duck
½ cup chopped onion
2 teaspoons sage
1 teaspoon pepper
1 tablespoon sausage
   seasoning
6 or 7 cups bread crumbs

1 cup chopped celery
⅓ cup bell pepper, chopped
3 eggs, beaten
1 teaspoon salt
Pinch sugar
Broth

Wash and cook duck in large pot with water and seasonings. Drop pieces of celery and onion into pot for flavor. Cook until done. Remove from broth and wrap in foil and bake. Take broth and make dressing. Precook green pepper, onion, and celery in a little oil. Then pour into seasoned bread crumbs. Stir and pour into pan and bake at 375 degrees until brown about 35 to 45 minutes.

COUNTRY RABBIT WITH SWEET POTATOES

1 to 2 pounds rabbit
1 teaspoon sage crumbs
Salt and pepper to taste
⅔ cup flour
¼ cup cider vinegar

3 teaspoons sausage
   seasoning
Juice of 1 lemon
4 or 5 small sweet potatoes

Clean and boil rabbit in large pot with a little salt added to the water. Cook until tender. Drain and season to taste. Coat with flour and sage and pour vinegar and lemon juice over opossum. Sprinkle sausage seasoning. Place raw sweet potatoes around opossum and bake until brown.

PORK CHITTERLINGS

10 pounds pork chitterlings	1 large onion, chopped
2 teaspoons red pepper	3 tablespoons vinegar
	Salt and pepper to taste

Wash chitterlings thoroughly. Remove some fat if there are dark spots on fat. Some fat must be left on chitterlings. Place chitterlings into a large pot; add water. Then season with vinegar, salt, red pepper and chopped onion. Cook for 4 hours over very low heat. Serve with cole slaw and hot sauce.

OXTAIL STEW

2 pounds oxtails	4 potatoes, cut in half
2 teaspoons salt	1 16-ounce can whole tomatoes
4 cups water	5 carrots, sliced
1 teaspoon pepper	
1 cup chopped onion	

Cut and wash oxtails. Put into pot with water. Add salt, pepper, and chopped onion. Cook until almost done. Add potatoes, tomatoes, carrots and finish cooking. If desired, sprinkle with red pepper. Cook 4 hours or longer over low heat.

FRIED RABBIT WITH BROWN GRAVY

1 rabbit, cut into pieces   1 teaspoon salt
1 teaspoon vinegar   1 cup flour
Water   ½ cup onion, chopped
1½ teaspoons pepper   Cooking oil

Soak rabbit overnight in salted water and vinegar. Wash in cold
water and pat dry. Add seasoning. Coat in flour and place in hot
oil. Fry until brown. Remove rabbit from oil; sprinkle some flour in
oil and let flour brown. Put rabbit back into skillet with chopped
onion. Add water. Stir and simmer on low heat until done.

SOUTHERN FRIED SQUIRREL

1½ pounds squirrel meat   1 teaspoon seasoned salt
1 teaspoon ground pepper   1 cup flour
1 teaspoon parsley flakes   1½ cups cooking oil

Boil squirrel until tender; remove from water; pat dry. Season and
coat with flour. Place into hot oil and cook until brown. If desired,
make brown gravy.

CORNISH GAME HEN

1 to 1½ pound Cornish
   game hen
1 teaspoon salt
1 teaspoon pepper
½ tablespoon vinegar
¼ teaspoon paprika

2 cups uncooked long grain
   wild rice
⅔ cup chopped onion
½ cup chopped celery
1 teaspoon green pepper

Wash hen; place hen into a roasting pan. Season with salt, pepper; pour vinegar over hen to make meat tender. Sprinkle paprika on hen and bake in oven. Occasionally baste with melted butter. Cover hen with foil until almost done then uncover to brown. Wash rice, then cook until done and fluffy. Simmer onion, celery in margarine until tender. Stir green pepper into rice along with onion and celery. Bake at 400 degrees for 1½ hours.

Sauce:

½ can chicken broth
2 tablespoons flour
¼ cup margarine

Salt and pepper
⅔ cup pineapple juice
2 tablespoons soy sauce

Combine all ingredients. Cook over low heat; stir until smooth and slightly thick. Place hen on platter; surround with rice. Pour sauce over hen and rice.

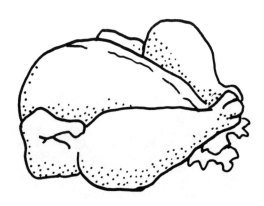

BAKED FISH FILLETS

3 pounds fish fillets
2 tablespoons lemon juice
1 stick butter, melted

2 teaspoons parsley flakes
1 small onion
Salt and pepper

Cut fillets into pieces, season with salt and pepper. Pour lemon juice and melted butter over fish. Sprinkle parsley flakes over fish. Make onion rings and lay on top of fish. Bake 25 minutes in 375 degree oven or until fish flakes easily. Serve hot.

FRIED FISH

3 to 5 pounds dressed fish
2 teaspoons pepper
¼ teaspoon paprika

1 tablespoon salt
½ teaspoon minced garlic
1¾ cup corn meal

Mix dry ingredients together in a paper bag. Put fish into bag and shake, place in hot oil and cook until golden brown. Serve with tartar sauce or cucumber sauce.

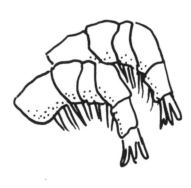

MACKEREL LOAF

2 16-ounce cans mackeral	1 teaspoon pepper
2 eggs	2/3 cup chopped onion
1/4 cup chopped green	1/4 cup chopped celery
pepper	1/2 can tomato sauce
1 cup cracker crumbs	1 cup mashed potatoes

Mix all ingredients together except 1/2 can tomato sauce. Shape into a loaf. Pour remaining 1/2 can tomato sauce over loaf. Cook for 25 minutes at 375 degrees. Spread potatoes over loaf and bake 10 more minutes until light brown.

FRIED OYSTERS

1 1/2 pints oysters	2 eggs
1 teaspoon pepper	3 cups corn meal
1 teaspoon seasoned salt	4 tablespoons milk

Wash and drain oysters. Season and roll over in corn meal. Dip into egg and milk batter and meal again. Drop into hot oil; fry for 1 minute on each side; place on paper towel to drain. *Serves 3 or 4.*

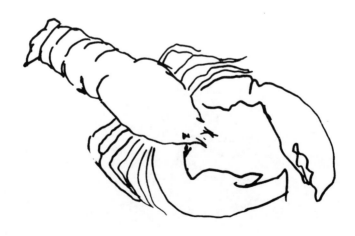

OYSTER DRESSING

2 pints oysters
1 can mushroom soup,
   diluted
5 cups bread crumbs
1 teaspoon seasoned salt
2 teaspoons ground pepper
½ teaspoon poultry
   seasoning

2 teaspoons sage
1 egg
2 tablespoons butter or oil
½ cup chopped onion
½ cup chopped celery

Heat oysters in mushroom soup and water for just a minute until heated through. Set aside. Simmer onion and celery in 2 tablespoons fat; then add to bread crumbs and seasonings. Add egg. Pour oyster broth gradually into bread crumbs mixing well to moisten dry ingredients. Pour into greased pan and bake at 350 degrees for 20-25 minutes until brown.

OYSTER STEW

3 pints oysters
½ cup butter
2 tablespoons flour
1 teaspoon salt

½ teaspoon pepper
4 cups milk
¼ cup Worcestershire sauce
½ teaspoon garlic powder

Wash oysters and remove any shell. Drain. Make a paste of butter and flour in skillet over medium heat. Add salt, pepper, and milk, stirring constantly. Add oysters, Worcestershire sauce and garlic salt. Cook until oysters are plump and their edges curl. Do not boil. Serve hot with oyster crackers.

SHRIMP COCKTAIL AND SAUCE

1 pound peeled, cooked
   shrimp
1 medium size can V-8 juice
1 teaspoon minced onion
1 teaspoon sugar
½ teaspoon parsley flakes

¼ teaspoon salt
Dash pepper
2 tablespoons lemon juice
½ teaspoon Worcestershire
   sauce
3 drops Tabasco sauce

To boil 1 pound of shrimp use 1 quart of water and 1 tablespoon salt. Boil shrimp in shell until done; peel. Combine all ingredients, except shrimp; stir and chill sauce before serving. To serve, center a dish with crushed ice on the table. Place shrimp around the edge of dish and put the sauce in a cup or bowl in the center of the shrimp.

FRIED SHRIMP

2 pounds raw shrimp
1 egg
1 cup milk
1 teaspoon pepper
1 cup yellow meal

1 teaspoon salt
¼ teaspoon parsley flakes
1 tablespoon flour
Oil for deep frying

Peel and devein shrimp. Dip into egg and milk batter, then into mixture of all dry ingredients. Drop shrimp into hot oil; cook until brown.

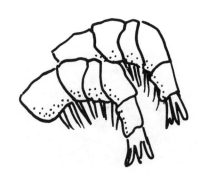

CUCUMBER SAUCE FOR FISH

1 medium cucumber
1 teaspoon white pepper
1 teaspoon minced onion
2 tablespoons mayonnaise

½ teaspoon salt
2 tablespoons mild vinegar
Pinch sugar
¼ teaspoon paprika

Wash and peel cucumber and finely chop. Mix all ingredients together except paprika which is sprinkled on last. Chill before serving. *Good with any kind of fish.*

SALMON CROQUETTES

1 can pink salmon
1 teaspoon ground pepper
1 egg

¼ teaspoon salt
¼ cup chopped onion
3 tablespoons flour

Pour salmon into bowl; combine with remaining ingredients and make patties. Place into hot oil and cook until golden brown.

Main Dishes

BEEF POT ROAST

2 or 3 pound roast
1 teaspoon pepper
1 teaspoon salt
¼ cup flour
1 can cream of onion soup
   or cream of mushroom
   soup

1 small onion, sliced
1 teaspoon garlic powder
1 tablespoon vinegar
½ cup diced carrots
2 large potatoes, quartered

Wash pot roast off; pat dry. Rub pepper, salt, and flour into meat. Place roast into greased skillet and brown on both sides; then add one cup cold water. Remove from heat; add onion soup, sliced onion, garlic powder, and vinegar. Cover roast and place in oven. Cook from 1½ to 2 hours according to weight of meat at 325 degrees. When roast is almost done, add vegetables and cook about 30 minutes longer.

BAKED BEANS AND FRANKS

1 large jar Boston baked
   beans
⅔ cup chopped onion
1 6-ounce can tomato paste

4 large franks
1 tablespoon sugar
Salt and pepper

Pour beans into casserole dish. Add tomato paste, sugar, and onions. Stir; salt and pepper to taste. Cut franks into 1 inch cubes and add to mixture. Stir; Bake at 350 degrees for 35-40 minutes. *Serves 4.*

OLD FASHIONED BAKED BEANS AND FRANKS

2 ½ cups dried northern
  beans
¼ cup molasses
¹/₈ cup brown sugar

½ teaspoon dry mustard
1 8-ounce can tomato sauce
3 franks, cut into round
  pieces

Combine dried northern beans, molasses, brown sugar, dry mustard, tomato sauce and cut franks. Salt and pepper to taste. Mix well and bake at 375 degrees for 25 to 30 minutes.

HUSH PUPPY

1 cup corn meal
1 cup flour
1 tablespoon sugar

10 hot dogs
Wesson oil
Prepared mustard

Mix meal and flour together with sugar. Pour enough water in to make batter stiff enough to adhere to the hot dog. Roll the hot dog in batter and drop into a skillet of hot Wesson oil until brown. *Serve with prepared mustard. Good for children after school.*

SPLIT WEINER WITH KRAUT

1 16-ounce can sauerkraut
1 pound weiners
3 cups water
Buns

Prepared mustard
¼ teaspoon pepper
Grated cheese (Optional)

Boil kraut in water and drain. Boil weiners and allow them to become puffy. Remove from water. Warm buns and spread with mustard. Add split weiner and kraut. Season to taste. Sprinkle cheese over top if desired.

CORNED BEEF AND CABBAGE

4 to 5 pound corned beef
   brisket
Little oil
1¼ tablespoon minced
   onion
¼ cup chopped celery
1 teaspoon seasoned
   pepper

1 teaspoon seasoned salt
2 bay leaves, crumbled
2 teaspoons garlic powder
1 teaspoon dry mustard
½ cup diced potato
1 small chopped cabbage
1 can tomato paste

Place corned beef in skillet with a little oil and brown on all sides. Add a little water and onion, celery, seasoned pepper, salt, crumbled bay leaf, garlic, and dry mustard. Cover with lid or foil and cook for 3 hours; then add potato, cabbage, and pour tomato paste over top of corned beef and cabbage. Sprinkle with paprika if desired. Let simmer for 30 more minutes with cover on. *Serves 7 or 8.*

SIRLOIN STEAK

1 sirloin steak, 2 inches thick	2 teaspoons salt
2 teaspoons ground pepper	1 teaspoon Italian seasoning
¼ teaspoon garlic powder	4 tablespoons Crisco oil

Cut all fat from steak; season on both sides. Place into hot oil and brown on both sides. Cook well done. Serve with steak sauce.

MINUTE STEAKS

4 minute steaks	1 teaspoon basil
2 teaspoons ground pepper	1 teaspoon garlic salt

Season steaks and coat them with flour. Place into hot oil; fry until brown and well done, about 4 minutes on each side. If you want gravy, remove steaks from oil and sprinkle flour into oil. Let flour brown. Then pour water into skillet and stir. Place steaks back into skillet with gravy and simmer for 10-15 minutes. Serve with creamed potatoes.

NEW YORK STEAK

1 New York strip steak, 2
   inches thick
2 teaspoons black pepper

1 teaspoon salt
½ teaspoon thyme

Wash steak; pat dry. Season on both sides. Place into hot oil in skillet and cook well done and brown on both sides. Remove fat from steak. Serve with Worcestershire sauce.

RIBEYE STEAK

1 steak, 1½ inches thick
1 teaspoon ground pepper
1 teaspoon salt

1 tablespoon Italian
   seasoning
1 tablespoon oil

Wash off; pat dry. Sprinkle seasoning on both sides. Place into hot oil and brown on both sides. Cook well done. Remove fat from steaks. Serve with baked potato, salad, cut beans, Pepsi-Cola and crackers.

BARBECUED SPARERIBS

5 pounds spareribs
2 teaspoons salt
3 tablespoons vinegar
⅔ cup finely chopped onion
1 teaspoon dry mustard
1 tablespoon sugar
2 cups water

2 teaspoons ground pepper
1 tablespoon Worcester-
    shire sauce
1 cup catsup
10 drops liquid smoke
¹/₈ cup lemon juice

Wash spareribs in salt water. Pat dry; cut spareribs into medium sized pieces. Place ribs into a large pan. Add seasonings and other ingredients. Cover ribs; put into oven and bake at 375 degrees for 1 hour and 45 minutes. *Makes 5 to 7 servings.*

T-BONE STEAK

1 T-bone steak
1 teaspoon salt

1 teaspoon oregano
1 teaspoon pepper

Wash steak off; pat dry. Cut all fat from steak. Season on both sides. Place into a little oil and brown on both sides. Cook until well done. Serve with French fries and combination salad.

BEEF AND NOODLES

1 pound beef short ribs	⅓ cup chopped onion
1 quart water	½ green pepper, diced
1 8-ounce package noodles	1 teaspoon parsley
1 teaspoon salt	1 garlic clove, crushed
1 teaspoon pepper	1 can whole peeled
1 teaspoon thyme leaves	tomatoes
1 teaspoon marjoram	1 8-ounce can tomato sauce
leaves	

Wash meat; put into a kettle with water; boil until tender. Combine all other ingredients and simmer until done; about 30 to 45 minutes.

SPARERIBS AND SAUERKRAUT CASSEROLE

3 pounds meaty spareribs	1 small jar chopped
2 quarts water	pimento, drained
½ teaspoon salt	1 large green pepper, cut in
Dash pepper	rings
1 15-ounce can sauerkraut,	1 can artichokes, drained
drained and rinsed	Tomato catsup

Cook ribs in water with salt and pepper until tender. (If meat comes off bone when tested with fork, it is done.) Drain ribs. Heat kraut in saucepan while ribs are cooking. Drain kraut. Turn oven on to 375 degrees to preheat. Place ribs in center of large casserole dish. Put kraut around ribs along with artichokes. Top with pimento and green pepper rings. Place in oven and bake for 25 minutes or until pepper rings are tender. *Serves 5 or 6. Serve with catsup.*

BEEF STEW

2 pounds beef stew meat
3 tablespoons fat
1 quart water
1 teaspoon pepper
½ cup chopped celery
1 teaspoon oregano
3 cups diced potatoes
1 cup diced carrots
1 10-ounce package frozen
　　green peas
1 teaspoon paprika
½ cup ketchup
1 teaspoon seasoned salt

1 small onion, chopped
⅓ cup diced green pepper
2 teaspoons minced garlic
1 can sliced mushrooms
1 10-ounce package frozen
　　cut okra
1 can whole kernel corn
2 cans whole peeled
　　tomatoes
2 8-ounce cans tomato
　　sauce
1 large package egg
　　noodles

Brown stew meat in hot fat. Add water and the rest of the ingredients. Cook until the meat and all vegetables are done about 1½ to 2½ hours over medium heat. Serve steaming hot with crackers. *Serves 12 or more.*

FLAME BEEF STROGANOFF

2½ pounds cubed beef
1 tablespoon flour
Salt and pepper
⅓ cup Wesson oil
¾ cup diced onion
1 cup sliced mushrooms
1 teaspoon minced garlic

½ cup cooked rice
1 can condensed tomato
  soup
2 cups sour cream
1 teaspoon dry white wine
Dry toast

Cut 2½ pounds tender beef into ¼-inch cubes. Coat with flour seasoned with salt and pepper. Heat skillet over flame, add Wesson oil, heat, and brown beef quickly on all sides. Add chopped onions, mushrooms, minced garlic, cooked rice, and stir in soup, sour cream and white wine. Simmer over low heat for 30 minutes. *Serve over dry toast.*

CHUCK ROAST

1 2 pound beef chuck roast
2 teaspoons pepper
2 teaspoons garlic salt
½ teaspoon meat tenderizer

1 tablespoon Worcester-
  shire sauce
¼ cup meat marinade
¼ cup wine vinegar

Season meat with pepper, garlic salt and meat tenderizer. Brown roast lightly on both sides in a skillet with a little oil. Remove to roasting pan. Pour meat marinade, wine vinegar, and Worcestershire sauce over meat. Cover and cook at 350 degrees for 1½ to 2 hours until tender.

CHEESEBURGER LOAF

1½ pounds ground beef
¼ cup chopped green onion
1 teaspoon ground pepper
½ teaspoon parsley
1 egg
3 tablespoons ketchup
¼ cup chopped onions
1 teaspoon season salt
1 cup cracker crumbs
¼ teaspoon dry mustard
½ cup sweet milk
4 slices American cheese

Mix all ingredients into meat except cheese. Put half the meat mixture into a loaf pan. Put 2 cheese slices on top, then another layer of meat and cheese. Bake in 350 degree oven for 45 minutes or until done. Allow loaf to set 10 minutes before removing from pan.

CHEESEBURGER SANDWICH

½ pound ground chuck
1 teaspoon thyme
Salt and pepper
1 slice tomato
1 lettuce leaf
1 slice onion
1 slice cheese
Mustard or mayonnaise

Work seasoning into ground chuck; make patties. Place into a little oil in skillet; cook until well done and brown. Warm buns, spread with mustard or mayonnaise. Add slice of tomato, onion, lettuce and cheese.

HAMBURGER STEAK WITH ONIONS

1½ pounds ground chuck
1 teaspoon pepper
1 teaspoon seasoned salt
1 slice wet bread
2 tablespoons chopped
  green pepper
1 teaspoon minced onion
1 large onion

Mix ground chuck, salt, pepper, bread, green pepper and minced onion. Shape into steaks. Place in pan and cook until well done. Slice onion and place over top of steaks. Cover skillet and continue cooking for a few minutes.

RED BEANS STROGANOFF

Little oil
1 pound ground beef
1 teaspoon seasoned salt
1 teaspoon lemon-pepper
1 clove garlic
2 teaspoons parsley flakes
¼ cup chopped green
   onions

1 10½-ounce can tomato
   soup
Tabasco sauce
1 cup sour cream
1 16-ounce can red beans

Put oil in skillet and add ground beef, salt, pepper, garlic, parsley, and chopped green onions. Let ground beef brown then add tomato soup, Tabasco sauce, and cook for 15 more minutes. Add sour cream and red beans. Cook an additional 15 minutes. *Serves 5 or 6. Serve with garlic bread or toast.*

CHILI WITH BEANS

1 pound ground beef
Little oil
¼ teaspoon salt
¼ teaspoon pepper
2 teaspoons chili pepper
⅓ cup chopped onion

¹/₈ cup chopped celery
1 package chili mix
1 can tomato paste
1 can whole tomatoes
1 can kidney beans
Tabasco sauce

Mix ground beef in skillet with a little oil and brown. Add salt, pepper, chili powder, onion, celery, and stir. Add chili mix, tomato paste, and whole tomatoes. Cook slowly, then add kidney beans. Simmer for about 30 minutes. For hot chili add a few drops Tabasco sauce.

CHILI WITHOUT BEANS

1 pound ground beef
Little oil
1 teaspoon seasoned salt
1 teaspoon pepper
¼ cup chopped celery
1 clove chopped garlic
1½ teaspoon chili powder

1 package chili mix
1 can tomato paste
1 can tomato sauce
½ bottle ketchup
Sliced mushrooms
Crackers

Mix ground beef with oil in skillet and brown. Add salt, pepper, chopped onion, pepper, celery, and garlic. Stir in chili powder and chili mix with a little water. Pour tomato paste, tomato sauce, and ketchup into mixture. Cook over low heat. If desired add sliced mushrooms.

GREEN CABBAGE ROLLS

1 medium-sized head
   cabbage
2 teaspoons sugar
¼ cup chopped parsley
1 teaspoon ground pepper
½ cup bread crumbs
1 cup bacon bits

⅓ cup bacon drippings
1 teaspoon salt
⅔ cup chopped onion
1 teaspoon paprika
1 pound ground beef
Cheese, to be melted

Wash cabbage and take larger leaves from it. Mix all other ingredients and roll some of the mixture up in the large cabbage leaves. Hollow out the rest of cabbage head and stuff with remainder of mixture. Place cabbage and cabbage rolls in covered casserole dish and bake at 325 or 350 degrees for 35 minutes. About halfway through, pour melted cheese and bacon bits over cabbage. Sprinkle with paprika.

STUFFED BELL PEPPERS

4 large bell peppers
½ pound ground beef
2 cups uncooked rice
1 teaspoon garlic salt

1 teaspoon pepper
¼ cup chopped onions
¼ cup tomato sauce

Core and clean out bell peppers; set aside. Combine ground beef, uncooked rice, salt, pepper, and onions. Mix in ½ of the tomato sauce. Stuff ingredients back into bell pepper and cook peppers in tomato sauce at 350 or 375 degrees until well done. If desired sprinkle cheese over top of each bell pepper.

MACARONI DINNER

1 package macaroni
1 teaspoon salt
1 pound ground beef
3 tablespoons corn oil
½ cup chopped onion
⅓ cup chopped green
   pepper
½ cup chopped celery

2 cups whole kernel corn
1 teaspoon pepper
1 can tomato paste
1 can tomato sauce with
   mushrooms
1 cup grated American
   cheese

Cook macaroni as directed on package. Brown ground beef in corn oil and add chopped onion, green pepper, chopped celery, drained whole kernel corn, salt, and pepper. Mix tomato paste and tomato sauce together and stir into macaroni. Pour all ingredients except grated cheese into casserole dish and sprinkle cheese on top. Bake in oven for 15 to 20 minutes and serve hot.

NOODLE CASSEROLE

1 8-ounce package egg
   noodles
2/3 cup onion, chopped
2/3 cup bell pepper, chopped
1 pound ground beef
4 tablespoons Mazola
   margarine
1 package (5-ounce) dry
   spaghetti mix

1/2 teaspoon salt
Dash curry powder
1/2 teaspoon pepper
2 15-ounce cans tomato
   sauce
1 cup Cheddar cheese,
   grated

Preheat oven to 350 degrees. Cook noodles according to package directions. Drain and set aside. Sauté pepper and onion in butter until tender but do not brown. Add ground beef and brown. Add remaining ingredients and simmer for 5 minutes. Grease two-quart casserole dish. Pour 1/2 meat sauce into casserole, cover with noodles, and pour on remaining sauce. Sprinkle with cheese. Bake at 350 degrees for 25-30 minutes. *Serves 6-8.*

POTATOES LASAGNE

1 1/2 pounds ground beef
Little oil
3/4 cup chopped onions
1/4 cup chopped celery
1/4 cup chopped green
   pepper
1 teaspoon salt
1 teaspoon pepper

2 cans tomato paste
1 tablespoon sugar
1 teaspoon basil leaves
1 teaspoon oregano leaves
1/4 teaspoon chopped garlic
1 cup sour cream
5 or 6 potatoes, thinly
   sliced

Combine ground beef in skillet with oil, onion, celery, green pepper, salt, pepper, tomato paste, sugar, basil leaves, oregano leaves and chopped garlic. Stir in sour cream. Simmer sauce on top of stove for 1/2 hour. Pour part of the sauce in bottom of pan, cover with a layer of sliced potato, and repeat until ingredients are all used. Bake at 400 degrees for 1 hour in covered pan. *Top with Parmesan cheese if desired.*

ITALIAN SPAGHETTI

1 pound ground chuck
1/2 cup onion, chopped
1/4 cup green pepper,
  chopped
1 clove garlic, minced
1/2 teaspoon salt
1/4 teaspoon pepper
1 tablespoon sugar

1/4 teaspoon chili powder
1 8-ounce can tomato paste
1 15-ounce can tomato
  sauce
2 tablespoons oil
1 12-ounce package
  spaghetti
Parmesan cheese, grated

Sauté onion and green pepper in oil until tender. Add ground chuck and brown. Drain off fat and add remaining ingredients except spaghetti and cheese. Cook sauce slowly while preparing spaghetti. Cook spaghetti according to package directions. Serve meat sauce over spaghetti and sprinkle Parmesan cheese on top. *Serves 5 or 6.*

GROUND BEEF CROQUETTES

1/2 pound ground beef
1 teaspoon seasoned salt
1 teaspoon pepper
1/4 cup chopped onion

1/4 cup chopped green
  pepper
3 tablespoons flour

Mix all ingredients together; shape into patties. Place into hot oil and brown on both sides. Remove from oil. Add flour and let it brown; then add water. Put patties back into skillet with gravy. Simmer until thick and brown. Serve with rice or hot biscuits.

RED EAGLE MEATBALL AND SPAGHETTI DINNER

1 16-ounce package
  spaghetti
1½ pounds ground chuck
½ cup chopped onion
1 teaspoon chopped garlic
Salt
Pepper
1 egg

1 tablespoon parsley flakes
¾ cup bread crumbs
¼ cup bacon oil
¼ teaspoon butter-flavored
  salt
1 8-ounce can tomato sauce
2 8-ounce cans tomato-
  vegetable juice

Cook spaghetti as directed on box. Drain. Mix ground chuck, onion, garlic, salt, and pepper. Then mix in egg, parsley flakes, and bread crumbs. Make balls and drop into medium hot oil. Lightly brown. Season spaghetti with butter-flavored salt, pepper, tomato sauce, and tomato-vegetable juice. Add meatballs to spaghetti, cover pan, and simmer over low heat. *Sprinkle Parmesan cheese on top if desired. Serves 6 or 7. This is the last meal Elvis ate.*

SUNDAY MEATLOAF

1 pound ground beef
1 teaspoon salt
1 teaspoon ground pepper
2 garlic buds, chopped
¼ cup chopped onion

3 slices bread
½ cup wheat germ
¼ cup chopped celery
2 eggs
1 can tomato juice

Combine ground beef with salt, pepper, chopped garlic, onions, bread, wheat germ, and celery. Beat eggs and mix into meat. Cook meatloaf in tomato juice. Cover and bake in oven at 375 degrees for 35 minutes.

OATMEAL-OLIVES MEAT LOAF

2 pounds ground chuck
1 teaspoon salt
1 teaspoon pepper
¼ cup chopped celery
⅓ cup chopped onion
¼ teaspoon chopped garlic

2 eggs
2 stuffed sliced olives
1½ cup oatmeal
1 can tomato paste
Mashed potatoes

Mix ground chuck, salt, pepper, chopped celery, onion, garlic, olives, oatmeal, and half of the tomato paste. Make loaf, place in greased pan, and pour remainder of the tomato paste over it. Bake at 375 degrees for 30 to 40 minutes. 10 minutes before finishing spread mashed potatoes over top and brown.

GROUND BEEF STOVE TOPPING STROGANOFF

1 pound ground beef
¾ cup diced onion
1 teaspoon salt
¼ teaspoon pepper
¼ cup green pepper
¹/₈ cup bacon fat
1 small can tomato paste

1 16-ounce can condensed
   tomato soup
1 cup sliced mushrooms
1 cup sour cream
¹/₈ teaspoon garlic salt
½ cup cooked rice
1 tablespoon white wine

Mix ground beef, onion, pepper, salt, and green pepper together. Put bacon oil into skillet. Add meat; let it brown lightly. Then add tomato paste, tomato soup, sliced mushrooms, sour cream, garlic salt, and rice. Stir. Add white wine last. Let simmer on low for 1 hour in skillet. Serve with toast.

PORK OR BEEF LIVER WITH ONIONS

1 pound liver
1 teaspoon seasoned salt
1 teaspoon paprika
2 teaspoons pepper

1 cup flour
1 medium onion, sliced
1 cup Crisco oil

Wash liver in cold water; pat dry. Season with pepper, paprika and salt; coat with flour. Place into hot Crisco oil and cook until brown. Remove from oil. Sprinkle a little flour into oil and let it brown with onions. Put liver back into skillet with onions. Add 1 cup cold water; stir and simmer for 5-10 minutes.

SMOKED SAUSAGE AND RICE-A-RONI

2 large links smoked
    sausage
1 small onion, diced
1/3 cup diced green pepper
1 cup chopped celery
Little oil
1 16-ounce can whole
    tomatoes

1 8-ounce can tomato sauce
4 cups chicken Rice-a-Roni,
    cooked
2/3 cup water
1/3 cup butter or margarine
1 teaspoon salt
1 teaspoon lemon-pepper

Skin smoked sausage and cut into parts. In a skillet mix sausage, onions, green pepper, and celery in a little oil and cook until tender; drain oil off. Add whole tomatoes and tomato sauce. Cook Rice-a-Roni as directed on box and mix other ingredients into rice and pour into a 2-quart casserole dish. Lay some of the smoked sausage on top. Bake at 275 degrees for 15 to 20 minutes.

OLD FASHIONED LASAGNE - SAUSAGE CASSEROLE

1 pound link sausage
1 cup chopped onion
1 cup chopped pepper
1 2½-ounce can sliced
   mushrooms
1 6-ounce can tomato paste
1 8-ounce can tomato sauce
1 teaspoon oregano
1 teaspoon basil

2 tablespoons sugar
½ teaspoon salt
¼ teaspoon pepper
½ cup Parmesan cheese
1 16-ounce carton cottage
   cheese
8 ounces Mozzarella
   cheese, grated
1 package lasagne noodles

Skin and crumble sausage into skillet. Sauté until browned. Add onion and pepper and cook an additional 3 minutes. Add next 8 ingredients and simmer about 30 minutes, stirring occasionally. While sauce is simmering, cook noodles according to package directions and cool. To assemble casserole, spoon about 1 cup sauce into bottom of a 13x9x2-inch casserole dish. Add a layer of noodles, a layer of cheeses; repeat layers in same order, ending with a layer of meat sauce. Sprinkle Parmesan cheese over all and bake at 375 degrees for 25 to 30 minutes. Cool for 15 minutes before serving. *Serves 6.*

CASSEROLE DINNER

2 12-ounce package
   spinach
4 cups boiling water
1 teaspoon salt
1¼ cup cooked long-grain
   rice
3 eggs, beaten

1 teaspoon lemon-pepper
¼ cup chopped onion
4 tablespoons butter
2 ounces sliced mushrooms
1 teaspoon paprika
½ cup chopped smoked
   sausage links

Cook spinach in boiling water with salt until tender and drain. Cook rice in 2 cups or more water until done and dry. Mix beaten eggs into spinach; add all remaining ingredients except Parmesan cheese. Pour into buttered dish and cook at 375 degrees for 20 minutes. Sprinkle top with Parmesan cheese if desired.

STUFFED PORK CHOPS

6 or 7 pork chops, thick
  enough to stuff
1 teaspoon curry powder
1 teaspoon seasoned salt
1 teaspoon ground pepper
2 red tart apples
Crisco oil

Wash pork chops. Pat dry. Sprinkle with seasoned salt, pepper and curry powder. Sear the chops in Crisco oil until lightly browned on both sides. Remove from oil, put into pan for baking. Make stuffing. Fill each chop with stuffing. Bake in oven until chops are good and tender — about 45 minutes to 1 hour at 400 degrees. Core apples and slice. Place apple slices on top of pork chops.

Stuffing:

⅓ cup chopped celery
1 cup minced onions
2 teaspoons parsley flakes
1 cup bread crumbs

Simmer celery and onion in a little oil; add parsley and bread crumbs and mix ingredients. Put about 2 tablespoons stuffing in each pork chop.

PORK ROAST

4 pound pork roast
3 teaspoons salt
2 teaspoons ground pepper
2 tablespoons vinegar
2 teaspoons sage

Wash pork roast; pat dry. Rub seasoning into meat; sprinkle sage and vinegar over roast. Wrap in foil, put in roasting pan and cook until brown and tender. Cook about 35-40 minutes per pound at 325 degrees.

FRIED PORK CHOPS

6 medium-sized pork chops
1 teaspoon pepper
1/2 teaspoon parsley flakes
1 1/2 cup flour

1 teaspoon salt
1/2 teaspoon paprika
1/3 cup Crisco oil

Wash pork chops and pat dry. Sprinkle with salt and pepper; let pork chops stand 5 or 6 minutes for meat to absorb seasoning. Coat in flour with paprika and parsley flakes mixed in. Place in hot oil and fry until golden brown.

SWEET AND SOUR PORK

2 pounds boneless pork cut
    into 1-inch cubes
2 eggs, well-beaten
1/3 cup all-purpose flour

3 tablespoons water
1 teaspoon salt
1 cup Chef Way shortening

In a medium bowl mix eggs, flour, water and salt until smooth. Add pork cubes into batter; coat well. Fry in shortening until lightly browned. Remove meat from oil. Mix with sweet and sour sauce; serve with hot rice.

Sweet and Sour Sauce:

1 tablespoon cornstarch
1/2 cup water
1/3 cup brown sugar
1 can pineapple chunks,
    undrained
1/4 cup chopped green
    pepper

1/3 cup chopped onion
1 clove garlic, minced
1 8-ounce can tomato sauce
1 tablespoon soy sauce
1/4 cup red vinegar

Dissolve cornstarch in water. Put in saucepan with remaining ingredients. Simmer about 15-20 minutes until thick, stirring often.

PORK EARS, FEET AND TAILS

2 pounds each pork ears,
   feet and tails
3 quarts water
4 tablespoons vinegar

2 teaspoons salt
2 crushed red peppers
Ground pepper to taste

Wash pork parts in salted water. Put into 3 quarts of water and cook with vinegar, salt and pepper. Cook over medium heat for 2½ hours or longer until tender. Remove from broth; season with ground pepper to taste. Cut into pieces and serve with hot sauce. Good with any vegetable.

CAULIFLOWER AND HAM

1 head cauliflower
¼ cup butter
4 cups diced ham
1 cup grated Mozzarella
   cheese
1 egg yolk
1 cup sour cream

2 tablespoons minced
   onion
1 tablespoon basil leaves
¼ tablespoon salt and
   pepper
1 teaspoon paprika

Cook cauliflower in boiling water for 8 minutes. Drain. Put butter into a dish and place one layer of cauliflower in bottom. Layer cauliflower and ham, then sprinkle with cheese. Beat egg and sour cream together, mix onion, basil leaves, salt, and pepper. Add to egg and sour cream mixture. Pour over layered cauliflower. Sprinkle paprika and cheese over top and dot with butter. Bake at 375 degrees until light brown, about 25 minutes.

HAM BONE DUMPLINGS

1 large ham bone or any amount of leftover baked ham	2 quarts water Salt and pepper

Simmer ham bone in water for 15-20 minutes. Season with salt and pepper.

Dumplings:

2½ cups flour	½ cup Crisco shortening
1 teaspoon salt	1 cup cold water

Combine all ingredients to make dough. Add more flour if needed to make dough easy to handle. Place dough on floured board and roll very thin. Cut dough into small pieces and drop into pot with ham. Cook about 20-25 minutes more.

HAM HOCKS WITH PINTO BEANS

4 ham hocks	1 whole onion
2 quarts water	Salt and pepper
1 pound pinto beans	½ tablespoon sugar

Put cold water in pot and add washed ham hocks. Pick and wash beans and add to pot, along with whole onion. Cook from 3 to 4 hours until beans are done. Add sugar after beans are cooked. *Serves 6 to 7.*

BAKED HAM WITH BEER

12 pound precooked ham
2 teaspoons cinnamon
5 or 6 maraschino cherries
½ box brown sugar

1 8-ounce can sliced
   pineapple
½ quart beer

Place ham in a large pan. Rub brown sugar and cinnamon into meat. Place pineapple slices and cherries on ham with toothpicks. Pour beer over ham and baste while baking. Bake about 2½ hours at 325 degrees.

BAKED LAMB SHOULDER ROAST

2 or 3 pound lamb shoulder
1 teaspoon crushed bay
   leaves
1 teaspoon pepper
¼ teaspoon rosemary

1 tablespoon sherry wine
1 tablespoon lemon juice
1 teaspoon seasoned salt
1 tablespoon minced garlic
2 tablespoons vinegar

Place lamb into a large roasting pan; then add liquids and seasonings. Cook about 30 minutes per pound at 325 degrees. Serve with mint sauce.

BREADED VEAL CHOPS

6 veal chops, 1-inch thick
1 teaspoon salt
1 teaspoon pepper
1 teaspoon curry powder

1 egg
²⁄₃ cup milk
1½ cups flour
²⁄₃ cup Crisco shortening

Remove extra fat from meat; rinse off veal with water; season to taste. Dip into milk and egg batter, then coat with flour. Place into medium hot oil and brown on both sides until done. If desired, serve with brown gravy.

BARBECUE SAUCE

½ bottle ketchup
1 8-ounce can tomato juice
2 teaspoons sugar
3 tablespoons vinegar
2 tablespoons lemon juice

½ cup butter
¼ cup chopped onion
1 tablespoon Worcester-
  shire sauce
2 teaspoons Liquid Smoke

Combine ketchup and tomato juice. Add sugar, vinegar, lemon juice, butter, chopped onion, Worcestershire sauce, and Liquid Smoke. Cook until thick, then let sauce simmer. Pour over meat.

CHEESE SAUCE

2 tablespoons margarine
2 tablespoons flour
¼ teaspoon salt
Dash pepper

1 cup milk
½ cup grated Cheddar
  cheese

Melt margarine in saucepan over low heat. Stir in flour, salt, and dash pepper. Add milk and stir until smooth. Add cheese and cook until thick. Serve hot over vegetables.

HOLLANDAISE SAUCE

1 cup hot white sauce   2 egg yolks, beaten
1 tablespoon cidar vinegar   2 tablespoons butter

When white sauce is cooked, remove from heat. Add vinegar, beaten egg yolks, and butter. If desired add lemon juice or a few drops of onion juice for flavor. Cook over heat until thick. Serve immediately.

MINT SAUCE FOR LAMB

If using fresh mint:
1 cup vinegar   Pinch garlic powder
8 sprigs fresh mint   1/3 cup sugar

Place vinegar in saucepan and allow to boil. Stir in finely minced mint. Sprinkle in garlic powder and sugar. Let stand for 30 minutes. Strain and pour over lamb before baking.

If preferred, try this variation:
3 teaspoons lemon juice   1 1/2 tablespoons flour
1 cup warm water   1 tablespoon vinegar
1/4 cup sugar   1 teaspoon onion juice
1/2 teaspoon rosemary
2 teaspoons melted
       margarine

Combine all ingredients. Cook over medium heat until thick and smooth. Pour over lamb shoulder and bake.

PIZZA SAUCE

1 8-ounce can tomato paste
½ cup ketchup
2 tablespoons Wesson oil
Salt
Pepper
1 teaspoon parsley flakes
2 tablespoons minced
onion

¼ cup chopped green
pepper
1 1½-ounce jar sliced
mushrooms
½ cup Mozzarella cheese,
grated
½ cup sliced pepperoni

Mix tomato paste and ketchup together; pour in pan. Add oil, salt, pepper, parsley flakes, and minced onion. Cook and stir. Add chopped green pepper, sliced mushrooms, and simmer. Pour sauce on pizza crust and add grated cheese and sliced pepperoni on top. Bake at 425 degrees for 30 to 35 minutes, until crust is brown.

BROWN GRAVY

¼ cup oil
¹/₈ cup flour
½ teaspoon salt
1 teaspoon pepper

⅔ cup cold water
2 teaspoons Worcestershire
sauce

Place oil in a skillet. Stir in flour, salt and pepper and cold water. Heat, stirring constantly, to brown flour. Add Worcestershire sauce. Stir and cook a few more minutes. Serve hot with meat.

EGG GRAVY

3 tablespoons bacon oil
2 tablespoons flour
½ teaspoon salt
½ teaspoon pepper

1 cup milk
1 teaspoon parsley flakes
1 tablespoon lemon juice
3 boiled egg yolks, mashed

Brown flour in bacon oil; add salt and pepper. Stir in milk, parsley flakes and lemon juice. Remove from heat. Stir mashed egg yolks into gravy. Serve hot with biscuits.

MILK GRAVY

3 tablespoons bacon oil
½ teaspoon salt
¼ cup flour

1 teaspoon pepper
1 cup milk

Heat bacon oil in skillet. Stir in flour, salt and pepper. Let flour brown; then stir in milk. Cook until thick and smooth. Serve with hot biscuits.

TOMATO GRAVY

¼ cup bacon oil
½ can tomato sauce
3 tablespoons flour

1 can whole peeled tomatoes
1 teaspoon salt
1 teaspoon pepper

Pour bacon oil into skillet and heat. Mix flour and tomato sauce and stir into bacon oil. Add whole tomatoes and mash tomatoes into gravy while cooking. Add salt and pepper. Stir often. Cook until smooth and thick. Serve over biscuits.

Vegetables

ASPARAGUS WITH CHEESE SAUCE

1 10-ounce package frozen
  asparagus

1 cup water
½ teaspoon salt

Bring water and salt to a boil. Add asparagus and cook 10 to 20 minutes or until tender. Remove from heat immediately and drain.

Cheese sauce:

¼ cup margarine
2 tablespoons plain flour
¼ teaspoon salt
Dash pepper

¼ cup milk
½ cup Cheddar cheese,
  grated

Melt margarine in saucepan over medium heat. Add flour, salt and pepper, stirring constantly to make a paste. Gradually add milk, stirring until smooth. Add grated cheese and stir until melted. Remove from heat. Serve over hot asparagus. *Serves 4.*

SPECKLED BUTTER BEANS

1 pound fresh butter beans
1 teaspoon salt
¼ pound salt pork meat

4 or 5 small whole potatoes
½ teaspoon pepper
Bacon grease if needed

Put beans into boiling water with salt pork meat. Cook for 2 hours and add potatoes to pot. Cook for ½ hour longer, to make sure beans and potatoes are well-done. If there is not enough oil from salt pork, then add some bacon grease to pot. *Serve with any kind of meat.*

CUT GREEN BEANS

1 quart fresh snap beans
2½ quarts water
¼ pound salt pork
1 teaspoon salt
½ teaspoon pepper

5 or 6 small whole
   potatoes, peeled
1 4-ounce jar pimento,
   chopped

Snap beans short and wash. Put about 2½ quarts water into pot with salt pork. Let boil for 5 minutes. Add beans, salt and pepper and cook for about 2 hours. Add whole potatoes and cook for 30 more minutes. If not enough fat from meat, add some bacon grease to season. Put pimento into pot last. Can be served with any meat.

STRING SPLIT BEANS WITH PIMENTO

3 cans split beans
¼ cup margarine or bacon
   grease
½ teaspoon salt

1 teaspoon pepper
1 package sliced almonds
¼ teaspoon vinegar

Pour beans into pot and add margarine or bacon oil, salt and pepper. Add sliced almonds, vinegar, and cook over medium heat for 15 minutes. Remove from liquid with a slotted spoon. *Serve with any meat.*

PICKLED BEETS

12 medium to large beets
1½ cups sugar
4 cups cider vinegar

2 teaspoons cloves
4 tablespoons allspice
2 pint size canning jars

Scrub beets clean, using cold water. Place beets in a large saucepan and cover with water. Cover pan, place over high heat and bring to a boil. Cook 30 minutes or until tender. Drain and cool under running water. Peel and slice. Combine sugar, vinegar, and spices in saucepan. Bring to a boil. Add beets and bring to a boil again. Simmer for 5 minutes. Sterilize jars in very hot water. Spoon hot beets into hot jars, leaving ½ inch air space at top. Pour vinegar mixture over beets. Place lids on jars and tighten to seal. *Makes about 2 pints.*

SWEET BEETS

5 large beets, sliced
1 quart water
1 cup vinegar
½ cup sugar

1 teaspoon celery seed
1 tablespoon ground
  allspice

Cook beets whole in 1 quart water until tender. Remove from heat. Run cold water over beets to cool enough to skin and slice. Let vinegar, sugar and spices cook together. Pour beets into hot spice; cook for 3 more minutes. Remove from heat and cool. *Good with meat or vegetable.*

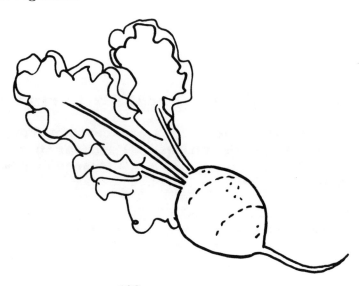

BROCCOLI AND CHEESE

2 10-ounce packages frozen
   broccoli
1 cup water
1 teaspoon salt

Dash pepper
⅓ cup bacon drippings
½ cup cheese sauce,
   warmed

Bring water and salt to a boil. Add broccoli and cook until tender, about 10 minutes. Drain. Sprinkle with pepper and bacon drippings or butter. Pour warm cheese sauce over broccoli and serve immediately. *Serves 4.*

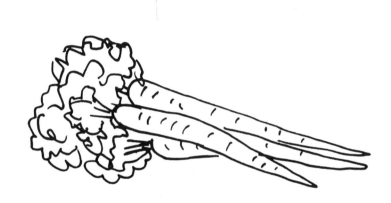

BRUSSELS SPROUTS

1 pound fresh Brussels
   sprouts
¼ cup bacon grease or
   ¼ pound pork meat
1 teaspoon pepper

1 teaspoon salt
½ cup cooked chestnuts,
   broken up
1 cup cheese sauce or sour
   cream

Wash sprouts thoroughly and cut off stems. Put water into pot with pork meat or bacon oil. Bring to hard boil for 5 minutes, then add Brussels sprouts. Cook until good and tender. Drain if desired, season to taste, and cover with cheese sauce or sour cream.

CABBAGE SPROUTS

2 bunches or 3 pounds
   cabbage sprouts
1½ quarts water

¼ pound smoked hog jowl
1 teaspoon salt
1 hot green pepper

Wash cabbage sprouts and cut stems short. Put water in pot with meat and let it boil; then add cabbage sprouts, salt, and cook for 2½ to 3 hours. Shortly before sprouts are done add 1 hot green pepper.

SMOTHERED CABBAGE

1 head cabbage, shredded
¼ cup onion, chopped
Small piece bacon fat
1 quart water

1 teaspoon salt
1 teaspoon sugar
Dash red pepper

Put bacon fat and water into skillet or large iron pot. Bring to a boil. Add cabbage, onion, salt and sugar. Cover pot or skillet and let cabbage cook low until tender. Sprinkle with red pepper before serving. *Serves 4 or 5.*

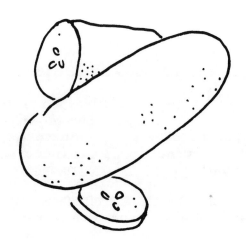

WHITE CAULIFLOWER CASSEROLE

1 medium-sized cauliflower
1 teaspoon salt
1 teaspoon pepper
2 tablespoons Mazola
  margarine
¼ cup pimento
½ cup bacon bits
½ cup grated Swiss cheese

½ cup cracker crumbs
1 15-ounce can cut green
  beans
2 drops Tabasco sauce
Paprika to taste
1 cup milk or 1 cup sour
  cream

Wash and trim cauliflower. Break into flowers and cook for 10 minutes. Remove and drain. Place into casserole dish and add salt and pepper and margarine. Mix all other ingredients together except Swiss cheese and add to casserole. If you use sour cream do not use flour. Sprinkle grated cheese over top of casserole and bake at 450 degrees for 20 to 25 minutes.

FRESH FRIED CORN

6 ears yellow or white corn
1 tablespoon flour
Salt and pepper to taste
Pinch sugar

¼ cup bacon drippings or
  butter-flavored oil
⅛ cup chopped green
  pepper

Cut corn off cob. Add milk, salt, pepper, pinch of sugar and flour, and stir corn with batter. Pour into hot oil. Stir and add green pepper. Continue to cook until done. *Serves 3 or 4.*

FRESH CORN PUDDING

6 ears fresh corn
1 15-ounch can cream style
corn
2 egg yolks
1 green pepper, chopped
2 teaspoons pimento,
chopped

¼ teaspoon paprika
2 tablespoons flour
1 teaspoon salt
Dash pepper
½ cup bacon grease

Preheat oven to 350 degrees. Cut corn off cob. If not juicy, add ½ cup water. Mix remaining ingredients with corn. Pour into buttered casserole dish. Bake in 350 degree oven for 45 minutes or until set. *Serves 8.*

FRIED CUCUMBER

½ inch thick cucumber
slices
1 tablespoon corn meal

2 tablespoons flour
Salt and pepper to taste
½ cup Crisco oil

Peel cucumbers and slice ½-inch thick. Mix meal and flour together; add salt and pepper to taste. Drop cucumbers into hot Crisco. Let cucumbers brown lightly. *Serve hot. You must love them to do this.*

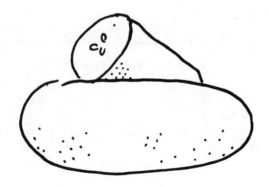

PLAIN DUMPLINGS

2 cups plain flour
1 teaspoon salt
½ cup Crisco

⅔ cup cold water
1 egg or ¼ teaspoon yellow
    food coloring

Sift flour into large mixing bowl. Add salt and Crisco. Add water a little at a time, mixing with fingers. Add egg or food coloring and work dough until it becomes stiff but is easy to handle. (All water may not be needed.) Sprinkle bread board with flour and turn dough out onto board. Roll very thin and cut into strips with knife to make dumplings. Dumplings may be used for potato dumplings or chicken and dumplings.

FRIED EGGPLANT

2 or 3 medium eggplants
1 teaspoon seasoned salt
1 teaspoon pepper
1 teaspoon paprika

1 cup flour
½ cup Chef-Way shortening
1 egg
1 cup milk

Wash eggplant and peel. Then slice and season with salt, pepper and paprika. Coat in flour and drip into hot oil. If desired, make a batter of egg and milk and dip eggplant in this before coating with flour. Fry until brown. *Serves 5 or 6.*

STUFFED EGGPLANT

2 large eggplants
¼ cup chopped celery
1 teaspoon salt
2 eggs
3 tablespoons bacon oil
⅓ cup chopped green
  onions
1 teaspoon lemon-pepper

1 teaspoon parsley flakes
½ teaspoon oregano
2½ cups cracker crumbs
1 can tomato sauce
1 cup grated sharp cheese
Few drops Tabasco sauce
  (Optional)

Boil eggplants whole in salted water until tender. Core them and remove the insides, retaining the pulp. Mix all ingredients together except cheese and half of the tomato sauce. Stuff the eggplant shells with this mixture. Pour the remaining tomato sauce over the eggplants and sprinkle with grated cheese. Bake at 350 or 375 for 30 minutes.

FRIED OKRA

1 10-ounce box cut okra
¼ teaspoon salt and pepper
Minced onions (Optional)

1 cup white corn meal
⅔ cup Crisco oil

Thaw frozen okra and season with salt and pepper. Add onions to meal and coat okra; Drop into hot Crisco oil. Cook until tender and brown. *Serves 1.*

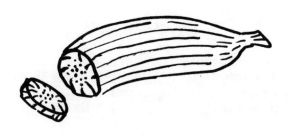

COLLARD GREENS (SOUL FOOD)

2 bunches collard greens
8 cups water
¼ pound pork meat or
    ½ cup bacon grease

Pinch baking soda
2 teaspoons salt
1 hot pepper

Wash collard greens and cut them into large pieces. Put water in large pot and add salt pork meat or bacon oil. Let water and meat come to a boil. Add cut collard greens. After cooking awhile, add pinch of soda to make collard greens tender. Add salt to taste. Add hot pepper to taste and cook 4 hours, less if collard greens are young.

SOUL FOOD MUSTARD AND TURNIP GREENS

3 bunches mixed greens
1 turnip, pared and sliced
3 quarts water
1 teaspoon salt

¼ pound salt pork
1 hot pepper
1 onion, sliced

Wash greens well several times in cold water. Rinse salt pork. Pour water into kettle and add salt and salt pork. Bring to boil and cook for 5 minutes. Add greens, stir down, and add more greens, until you have the amount you want to cook. Let greens cook for 3 hours or more. Add turnip slices 30 minutes before greens are done. Drop hot pepper in the last minute and cook for 3 minutes more. Remove from stove. Serve with onion slices and hot corn bread.

LIMA BEANS AND MUSHROOMS

2 cans lima beans or
   1 quart fresh beans
1 quart water
Salt and pepper
¼ cup bacon drippings
1 2½-ounce can mushrooms

1 can whole kernel corn
1 tablespoon flour
1 small jar whole sweet
   onions
1 small jar chopped pimento
1 hard-boiled egg

If using fresh lima beans, combine in a large kettle with 1 quart water, salt and pepper to taste, and cook for 2½ hours. If using canned lima beans add 1 can of water, salt, and pepper. Then add bacon drippings, mushrooms, whole kernel corn, and mix with flour. Add sweet onions, chopped pimento and boiled egg. Simmer over low heat until done.

LIMA BEANS WITH RICE

¼ pound salt pork
1 pound fresh lima or
   butter beans
1 quart cold water
1 teaspoon pepper

1 teaspoon salt
1 cup rice
1 2½-ounce jar chopped
   pimento

Shell beans and wash. Put into heavy saucepan along with salt pork, salt and pepper. Cook until almost done, about 1 hour. Add rice and pimento and cook 30 more minutes. *Serves 8.*

FRIED OKRA

1 pound fresh okra
½ teaspoon salt
½ teaspoon pepper
¼ teaspoon garlic salt

1 egg, slightly beaten
1 tablespoon flour
¾ cup corn meal
Hot oil

Wash and cut fresh okra in small pieces. Season with salt, garlic salt, and pepper. Mix flour with corn meal. Dip cut okra into beaten egg, then into corn meal mixture. Drop into 1 cup hot oil and fry until tender and brown. *Serves 2 to 4.*

FRIED ONION RINGS

4 to 5 large onions
1 egg
1 cup milk
1 cup flour

1 teaspoon garlic and
    parsley salt
1 cup Wesson oil

Slice onions and separate into rings. Make a batter of the beaten egg and milk. Sift together flour and seasoned salt; dip onions in flour and then in batter. Drop onion ring into hot Wesson oil and cook until golden brown. *Serve hot.*

STUFFED ONIONS

8 large onions
1 teaspoon salt
2/3 cup chopped celery
2 1/2 tablespoons chopped
   parsley

3 tablespoons margarine
3 cups bread crumbs or
   cooked rice
1 teaspoon pepper
1/2 cup bacon bits

Skin the onions, cut in half, and simmer in salt water until almost tender. Drain, and remove the center without disturbing the outside shell. Chop up the onion centers into fine pieces. Simmer celery and parsley in melted margarine until tender. Mix in crumbs. Add other ingredients. Mix well, then stuff back into onion shells. Put in a covered dish, and bake at 275 degrees for about 25 minutes or until light brown. Remove cover to brown at end of baking time.

GRANDMA'S FRIED ONIONS WITH EGGS

1 1/4 cups green onion,
   finely chopped
3 eggs, beaten

3 tablespoons butter
Salt and pepper to taste

Pour 1 cup water into skillet and bring to a boil. Add onion and cook slowly until tender. Drain water off, add butter and eggs. Cook and stir until eggs are desired doneness. Remove to plate and salt and pepper to taste. Serve immediately with hot biscuits.

CROWDER PEAS

2 15½-ounce packages   Pepper to taste
   crowder peas, frozen   1 sliced tomato
2 tablespoons bacon oil   1 diced onion
Pinch of salt

Pour peas into small kettle, add little water, bacon grease and season to own taste. Cook for about 25 minutes. Stir, spoon out. Use spoon with holes. Serve with tomatoes and diced onions. *this can be made with fresh or frozen peas. If fresh peas are used they need to be cooked for at least 2½ to 3 hours.*

GREEN BLACK-EYED PEAS

1 16-ounce package fresh   ¼ pound pork meat or
   green peas   bacon grease
3 quarts boiling water   1 small onion, chopped
1½ teaspoons salt   1 hot pepper

Pour green peas into boiling water and add salt, bacon grease or pork meat, onion, and hot pepper. Cook for 3½ hours or longer. Serve with sliced onion and tomato. Good with any kind of meat.

PURPLE HULL PEAS

1 pound dried peas
¼ pound salt pork, rinsed
1 teaspoon salt

2½ quarts water
1 pod hot pepper

Wash and pick peas and put on to boil with salt pork and salt. Cook for 3½ hours or until done. Drop hot pepper in few minutes before serving. *Serves 6-8.*

SOUTHERN FRIED PURPLE HULL PEAS

2 cups cooked leftover peas
1 cup flour
1 small onion, chopped

Salt and pepper
⅔ cup Crisco oil

Stir leftover peas, flour, and onion together in bowl. Season with salt and pepper. Make into patties. Pour oil into skillet and heat. Brown patties in hot oil on both sides. Serve hot.

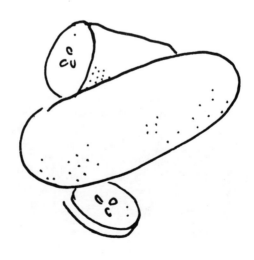

COUNTRY-STYLE FRENCH FRIES

5 or 6 large Irish potatoes   Dash pepper
1 teaspoon salt   2 cups Wesson oil

Peel potatoes. Cut into large French fries. Rinse often and pat dry with paper towel. Heat Wesson oil in heavy iron skillet or deep fat frier. Drop in potatoes and cook until golden brown. Remove from oil, drain on paper towels and sprinkle with salt and pepper. Serve hot. *Serves 1 or 2.*

HOME FRY IRISH POTATOES

6 or 7 large potatoes   1 teaspoon onion pepper
2 cups Crisco oil   1 teaspoon seasoned salt

Peel potatoes and rinse off under cold water. Slice them ½-inch thick and round, and season to taste. Heat Crisco oil until it is very hot. Remove from heat, place potatoes in oil, and cook until they are golden brown. Drain potatoes on paper towels. Wrap them in foil for 3 minutes to steam soft. *Serves 3.*

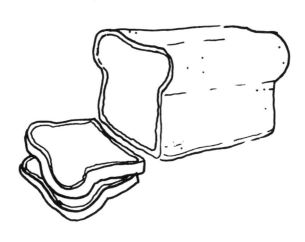

HASH BROWN POTATOES

3 or 4 boiled potatoes
2 tablespoons flour
3 tablespoons milk

¼ cup grated onion
1 teaspoon seasoned salt
1 teaspoon pepper

Let potatoes boil in jacket until cooked through. Drain and cool until potatoes are easy to handle. Grate potatoes lengthwise and season to taste. Stir in flour, milk, grated onion. Press into the shape of a square. Place into hot oil and brown. *Serves 1 or 2.*

MASHED POTATOES

6 medium potatoes
½ cup soft butter
½ teaspoon salt

¼ teaspoon lemon-pepper
⅓ cup milk
1 tablespoon parsley flakes

Wash and peel potatoes. Cut and dice; cook until tender. Drain and mash, add butter, salt, pepper, milk, and parsley flakes. Put into double boiler until ready to serve.

FRIED RICE

3 tablespoons shortening
⅓ cup chopped green
   pepper
¼ cup chopped onion
2 cups cooked rice

¼ teaspoon lemon-pepper
1 teaspoon salt
1 teaspoon parsley flakes
1 egg, beaten

Sauté onion and green pepper in shortening until tender. Add rice, lemon pepper, salt, parsley flakes, and beaten egg. Fry, stirring constantly, until egg is cooked and rice is hot. Serve immediately. *Serves 2 or 3.*

RICE DINNER MANHATTAN

2 cups Riceland rice,
   uncooked
3 cups water
3 tablespoons butter
1 teaspoon curry powder

1 cube chicken bouillon
1 small chopped onion
Little oil
1 2½-ounce can sliced
   mushrooms

Pour rice into cold water and cook with butter, lemon pepper, curry powder, and beef bouillon. Fry onion in vegetable oil but do not brown; cook just enough to flavor the rice. Pour into rice. Stir in mushrooms. Simmer. *Serves 4 to 5.*

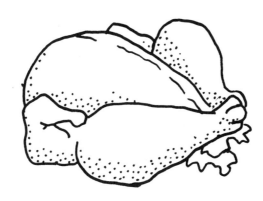

IRISH POTATO PUDDING

7 or 8 large potatoes	½ cup onions
1 teaspoon salt	½ cup milk
½ cup margarine	1 cup sour cream
1 teaspoon seasoned	Bacon bits
pepper	Grated cheese

Peel and dice potatoes, rinse off with cold water, and cook in about 1 quart of salted water. Cook until tender. Drain water off. Add margarine, salt, pepper, onions, milk, and sour cream and bacon bits. If desired sprinkle cheese over top and stir until creamy smooth. Pour into casserole dish and cook at 450 degrees for 20 to 25 minutes.

STUFFED BAKED POTATOES

4 or 5 Irish potatoes,	1 teaspoon salt
already baked	1 teaspoon pepper
3 tablespoons butter	Sprinkle of cheese and
1 cup minced onions	paprika
1 teaspoon parsley flakes	

Core inside of potatoes out and mash. Season with butter and other ingredients. Stuff back into hull and sprinkle grated cheese and paprika on top. Bake at 375 degrees for 10 minutes or long enough to let cheese melt down into potatoes. *Serve hot.*

POTATO DUMPLINGS

5 or 6 potatoes
1 teaspoon salt
¼ teaspoon pepper
⅓ cup bacon grease or
   margarine

½ teaspoon parsley flakes
*Dumplings

Peel and quarter potatoes. Put into a large pot along with 1 quart water. Add salt, pepper, parsley flakes, and bacon grease or margarine. Cook potatoes until they test-tender with a fork. Prepare 1 recipe dumplings while potatoes are cooking. Drop dumplings into pot with boiling potatoes, cover, and cook for 15 minutes. *Serves 4.*

See separate recipe for plain dumplings on page 111.

LEFTOVER POTATO PATTY FRY

Leftover mashed potatoes
⅓ cup chopped onion
½ teaspoon seasoned salt
½ teaspoon pepper

½ teaspoon parsley flakes
⅓ cup flour
¼ cup margarine or bacon
   grease

Combine mashed potatoes, onion, salt, pepper and parsley flakes. Shape into patties and coat both sides in flour. Melt margarine in skillet over medium high heat. Brown patties in margarine on both sides. Serve for breakfast with scrambled eggs.

ENGLISH PEA CASSEROLE

2 pounds fresh peas   1 quart water
1 teaspoon salt

Shell peas and wash. Put into saucepan with salt and water and cook low until done.

Casserole:

Peas   1 2½-ounce can sliced
1 cup sour cream   mushrooms
1 2½-ounce jar chopped   ½ cup onions, chopped
   pimento   1 teaspoon salt
3 or 4 potatoes, peeled and   Dash pepper
   diced

Mix all ingredients well and pour into buttered casserole. Bake 30 minutes at 325 degrees. *Serves 6-8. If desired, place sliced boiled eggs on top last 5 minutes of cooking.*

MASHED SWEET TURNIPS

5 or 6 medium turnips   Pinch salt
2 tablespoons margarine or   2 tablespoons sugar
   bacon grease   3 cups water
¼ teaspoon pepper

Rinse turnips well, peel, and slice. Put into pot with water. Add margarine or bacon grease, pepper, salt. Bring to a boil. Cook 15 to 20 minutes over low heat. Add sugar and cook until turnips are soft. Mash and season to taste. Serve hot. *Serves 4.*

MASHED RUTABAGAS

2 medium-sized rutabagas
½ cup turnips, diced
½ teaspoon salt
1 teaspoon pepper

2 tablespoons sugar
¼ cup Mazola margarine
4 cups water

Peel rutabagas and rinse under cold water. Slice and mix with turnips. Put into a large pot with salt, pepper, sugar, margarine, and water. Cook slowly until tender. Stir as needed. *Serves 2.*

BAKED SAUERKRAUT

2 15½-ounce cans chopped
  sauerkraut
1 teaspoon seasoned
  pepper
½ teaspoon salt
1 large can sliced
  mushrooms

½ cup sour cream
¼ cup salad oil
1 pound smoked sausage
  links

Wash chopped sauerkraut under running cold water. Pour into a 2-quart casserole dish and sprinkle with pepper and salt. Drain sliced mushrooms and add sour cream, salad oil, and skinned and cut sausage links over top of sauerkraut. Cover and bake at 400 degrees for 25 minutes.

THE GREEN EAGLE DISH WITH EGGS

1 can chopped spinach
3 tablespoons bacon grease
1 teaspoon salt
1 teaspoon seasoned pepper

¼ cup chopped onion
2 whole eggs, slightly
  beaten

Cook spinach until all water is gone. Add grease, salt, pepper, stir in onions and let spinach cook dry. Add eggs last. *Serves 1.*

FRIED SQUASH

6 or 7 yellow crookneck
  squash
½ cup chopped onion
1 cup water

1 teaspoon salt
½ teaspoon pepper
⅔ cup bacon grease

Wash squash and cut off ends; slice. Put squash, onion, water, salt and pepper into saucepan. Cook until tender. Drain off any excess water. Heat bacon grease in skillet. Add squash and cook until lightly browned. *Serves 3 or 4.*

SQUASH CASSEROLE

6 or 7 yellow summer
 squash
1 large onion, chopped
1 egg
½ cup margarine, softened
 to room temperature

1 teaspoon salt
1 teaspoon lemon-pepper
2 cups cracker crumbs
½ cup crumbled bacon

Wash squash and slice. Put into pot with a little water. Add onion and boil till tender. Drain. Preheat oven to 350 degrees. Mix squash with egg, margarine, salt, pepper and cracker crumbs. Pour into buttered casserole. Sprinkle bacon crumbs on top. Bake at 350 degrees for 20-25 minutes, or until lightly browned. *Serves 4-6.*

May substitute dry onion soup mix for onions.

FRIED GREEN TOMATOES

6 or 7 green tomatoes
Salt and pepper
1 cup plain flour

½ cup self-rising corn meal
1 cup Crisco oil

Slice unpeeled tomatoes ½-inch thick, and salt and pepper them. Mix flour and meal together and dip tomatoes in the mixture, then drop into very hot Crisco oil. Cook until tender and brown. *If you love tomatoes you will love these! To batter, dip tomatoes in an egg and milk mixture before coating them.*

Cakes

EASY AMBROSIA CAKE

2 boxes Duncan Hines cake
   mix
2 teaspoons baking powder
Pinch salt
2 1/2 cups milk
1/4 cup butter
4 eggs

1 teaspoon nutmeg
1 teaspoon vanilla
1 cup white raisins
1/2 cup chopped nuts
1 cup coconut, grated
1 cup grated orange rind

Pour cake mixes into a large bowl. Add baking powder, pinch of salt, milk, eggs, and butter. Add nutmeg, vanilla and stir raisins, chopped nuts, coconut and orange rind in with rest of ingredients. Pour into greased and floured cake pans. Bake at 350 degrees for 30 minutes to 1 hour. *Makes 3 layers.*

APPLESAUCE CAKE

1 egg
1 1/3 cups sugar
1/2 cup butter
2 1/2 cups cake flour
1 teaspoon soda
1/2 teaspoon salt

1 teaspoon ground cloves
1/2 teaspoon cinnamon
1 cup seedless raisins
1 1/3 cups thick unsweetened
   applesauce

Mix egg, sugar, and butter. Add flour, soda, spices and salt together. Beat until smooth. Then add chopped seedless raisins. Now add your unsweetened applesauce. Pour into greased and floured cake pan. Bake at 350 degrees for 30 minutes.

APRICOT CAKE

1 box Duncan Hines yellow
  cake mix
1 box raspberry Jello
½ cup milk
2 eggs, separated

½ cup margarine
1 cup mashed apricots
1 teaspoon pineapple
  flavoring

Combine cake mix and Jello together in a large bowl. Add milk, egg yolks, margarine; beat batter smooth, then add mashed apricots, pineapple flavoring. Stir. Beat egg whites until fluffy and fold into batter. Pour into greased and floured cake pan. Bake at 375 degrees for 40 minutes.

BANANA CAKE

2 eggs
2 cups sugar
½ cup margarine
4 cups flour
Pinch salt

1 teaspoon baking powder
½ cup milk
3 large mashed bananas
1 teaspoon banana
  flavoring

Blend eggs, sugar, butter together. Sift flour, salt, baking powder, Add milk. Beat batter until smooth. Add mashed banana and banana flavoring. Stir again. Pour into greased and floured pan. Bake at 350 degrees for 30 minutes.

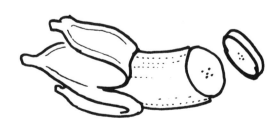

MIDNIGHT BLACKBERRY JAM CAKE

4 eggs
¾ cup butter
1 ¼ cups sugar
⅔ cup buttermilk
3 ½ cups plain flour
3 teaspoons baking powder

1 teaspoon soda
Pinch salt
1 teaspoon cinnamon
1 ½ cups blackberry jam
2 teaspoons rum flavoring

Combine eggs, sugar, butter; beat until smooth. Add milk. Sift flour, baking powder, soda, pinch of salt, and cinnamon. Stir into egg mixture. Add blackberry jam and rum flavoring. Pour into greased and floured cake pan. Bake at 350 to 375 degrees for 30 to 40 minutes.

CHEESECAKE

2 eggs
⅔ cup sugar
1 8-ounce package cream
   cheese

Pinch salt
1 teaspoon vanilla
1 cup sour cream
1 teaspoon cinnamon

Filling:
Combine eggs, sugar, softened cream cheese, salt, cinnamon, vanilla, and sour cream; beat until smooth.

Crust:
¼ cup melted butter
⅓ cup sugar

2 cups graham cracker
   crumbs

Mix graham cracker crumbs with butter and ⅓ cup sugar. Press into pie dish. Pour cake filling into crust. Bake at 350 degrees for 25-30 minutes. Sprinkle graham cracker crumbs over top.

LAZY CHERRY CAKE

1 egg
1 cup sugar
⅓ cup margarine
1 cup flour
¼ teaspoon salt

1 teaspoon baking powder
2 teaspoons vanilla
1 can cherry pie filling
½ cup chopped nuts

Beat egg, sugar, butter, flour, salt, and baking powder together. Stir ingredients well. Add flavoring; fold in cherry pie filling and chopped nuts. Pour into greased and floured cake pan. Bake at 350 degrees for 30 minutes.

UNDERBAKED COCONUT CAKE

4 eggs, separated
1 cup sugar
2 cups milk
Pinch salt
2 tablespoons flour
1 envelope unflavored
  gelatin
½ cup warm water

½ cup melted margarine
1 cup coconut cream
1 cup grated coconut
1 teaspoon vanilla
1 10-inch Angel Food cake,
  broken into pieces
Cool Whip

Beat egg yolks, sugar, milk, salt and flour. Stir in dissolved gelatin in ½ cup warm water. Cook over low heat until thick. Add melted margarine, coconut cream, grated coconut, and vanilla. Cool custard. Beat egg whites stiff; then fold into custard. Break cake into pieces; pour custard over pieces of cake and sprinkle top with coconut flakes and Cool Whip. Keep in refrigerator.

CHOCOLATE CAKE AND ICING

Cake:

4 ounce bar sweet
   chocolate
½ cup boiling water
3 eggs
2 cups sugar
½ cup margarine

3 cups all-purpose flour
1 teaspoon soda
1 teaspoon baking powder
Pinch salt
1 cup buttermilk
2 teaspoons vanilla

Melt chocolate in hot water. Combine eggs, sugar, and butter. Mix well. Add flour, soda, baking powder and salt. Stir in melted chocolate and milk. Beat batter until smooth. Add vanilla. Pour batter into greased and floured 9-inch cake pans. Should make 2 or 3 layers. Bake at 350 degrees for 35-40 minutes.

Icing:

1 cup Pet milk
½ cup cocoa
3 cups powdered sugar
¼ cup margarine

¼ teaspoon cream of tartar
Pinch salt
1 teaspoon vanilla

Warm milk; stir in cocoa and sugar. Stir in melted margarine, cream of tartar, salt, and vanilla. Beat until thick and smooth. Heat for 3 minutes, then remove from heat. Spread on cake.

DELICIOUS CAKE

5 eggs
1 pound brown sugar
Pinch salt
1 cup margarine
4 cups cake flour

2 teaspoons baking powder
1 box white raisins
¾ cup whiskey
⅔ cup chopped nuts

Mix all ingredients; beat batter until smooth. Add whiskey and nuts last. Pour into greased and floured cake pan. Bake at 350 degrees for 40 to 45 minutes. *Makes 2 layers.*

44 KARAT CAKE

2¾ cups cake flour
2 teaspoons baking powder
1 teaspoon baking soda
1 teaspoon nutmeg
2 teaspoons cinnamon

2 cups sugar
1½ tablespoons margarine
3 eggs
3 cups carrots, cooked
3½ tablespoons water

Sift flour, baking powder, soda, nutmeg, cinnamon together. Add sugar, margarine and eggs. Add pre-cooked carrots and water. Beat; add chopped nuts. Pour into greased and floured pan. Bake at 350 degrees for 30 minutes or longer.

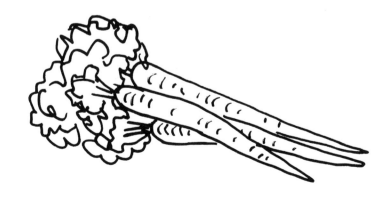

FRUITCAKE FOR THE HOLIDAY

4 eggs
½ cup butter
1 teaspoon vanilla
1 cup milk
1½ cups brown sugar
Pinch salt
2½ cups all-purpose flour
2 teaspoons baking powder
2 cups candied mixed fruit
1 teaspoon nutmeg

½ teaspoon allspice
1 teaspoon cinnamon
1½ cups chopped dates
½ cup chopped candied
  pineapple
1 cup chopped candied
  cherries
1 cup white raisins
½ pound pecan halves

Mix all ingredients into a large bowl. Beat eggs well, add butter, milk, brown sugar, vanilla and salt. Stir until moist. Then add flour and baking powder. Stir in mixed fruit, nutmeg, ground allspice, cinnamon, and all other candied fruits and nuts. Pour into tube pan with heavy wax paper in bottom of pan. Bake at 275 to 300 degrees for 1½ hours. Decorate cake top with red and green cherries and pecan halves. If you want a glazed look, pour a little white corn syrup over cake. Fruit cake should be cooked at least 6 months before the holiday, so it will have time to absorb natural flavor from fruits. Cake can be sprinkled once a month with your favorite rum. Keep it tightly wrapped in a cool place.

PRESSED NO-COOK FRUITCAKE

1 cup milk
2 pounds miniature
    marshmallows
1 cup chopped dates
1 ½ pounds seedless raisins
1 6-ounce package dried
    fruit

4 cups chopped nuts
2 cups candied mixed fruit
½ cup cherries, candied
2 teaspoons rum flavoring
1 ½ pounds graham cracker
    crumbs

Heat milk and marshmallows over low heat. Stir until marshmallows melt; remove from heat. Pour into a large bowl. Add fruits and nuts, and rum flavoring. Work in graham cracker crumbs with hands, mix well. Press fruitcake into a large tube pan. Let it set for 2 days in a cool place. Cover top with green and red candied cherries and nuts. Sprinkle cake with rum. Wrap tightly so cake won't lose its moisture. May be frozen or kept in refrigerator until the holidays.

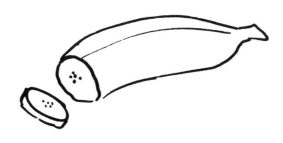

OLD FASHIONED MOLASSES TEACAKES

4 cups plain flour
1 teaspoon baking soda
1 teaspoon ginger
2 teaspoons baking powder
½ teaspoon salt

1 teaspoon nutmeg
½ cup pure lard
¼ cup water
2 eggs
1 cup molasses

Mix all dry ingredients together; then add lard, water, egg, and molasses. Stir; add more flour, if needed, to make stiff dough. Sprinkle cutting board with flour; place your dough and roll ½ inch thick. Cut into shape of a biscuit. Place on a greased cookie sheet. Bake in oven at 375 degrees until light brown — about 15-20 minutes.

COCONUT POUND CAKE

6 eggs
2½ cups sugar
2 cups butter
3 cups self-rising flour

1 cup milk
½ cup sour cream
1 teaspoon vanilla
½ cup coconut cream

Beat eggs well; add sugar, butter, flour, milk, sour cream, vanilla, and coconut cream. Mix well. Pour batter into greased and floured tube pan. Bake at 350 degrees for 1 hour.

PINEAPPLE-UPSIDE DOWN CAKE

2 boxes Duncan Hines
     white cake mix
⅔ cup margarine
4 eggs
1¾ cups milk

1 teaspoon vanilla
⅓ cup brown sugar
6 or 7 maraschino cherries
1 can sliced pineapple

Mix all ingredients, except brown sugar, sliced pineapple and cherries. Put those 3 at the bottom of pan. Pour smooth batter on top of pineapple. Bake at 350 degrees for 40-45 minutes. Let cool before removing from pan.

DATE POUND CAKE

6 eggs
¾ cup milk
2 cups margarine
3 cups self-rising flour

1 pound powdered sugar
Pinch salt
1 teaspoon vanilla
⅓ cup chopped dates

Beat eggs; add remaining ingredients. Mix well; pour into greased pan. Bake at 350 degrees for 1 hour or until done.

RED DEVIL CAKE

3 eggs
1 cup butter
1 ⅔ cups sugar
3 ½ cups plain flour
3 teaspoons baking powder

1 teaspoon soda
1 cup buttermilk
1 cup cocoa
2 drops red food color
2 teaspoons vanilla

Mix all ingredients with electric mixer or by hand until batter is smooth. Pour into greased and floured cake pans. Makes 2 layers. Bake 40 minutes at 350 degrees.

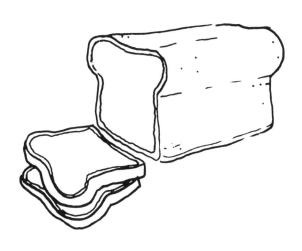

SOUR CREAM CAKE

1 package yellow cake mix
¼ cup milk
4 eggs
¼ cup sugar
½ cup margarine

1 cup sour cream
2 tablespoons brown sugar
1 cup chopped nuts
1 teaspoon vanilla

Mix in a large bowl: cake mix, milk, eggs, sugar, and margarine. Beat until smooth. Then add sour cream, brown sugar, and vanilla and chopped nuts. Beat batter smooth and pour into greased cake pan. Bake at 350 degrees for 20 to 30 minutes.

STRAWBERRY CAKE

4 cups cake flour
2 teaspoons baking powder
Pinch salt
1 cup milk

1 cup mashed strawberries
2 eggs
5 tablespoons butter,
   melted

Sift dry ingredients together. Add milk and eggs, strawberries and butter. Beat batter until smooth and creamy. Pour batter into greased and floured cake pans. Bake at 350 degrees for 30 minutes. *Makes 2 layers.*

SWEET POTATO CAKE

1 ½ cups Crisco oil
4 eggs, separated
2 cups sugar
4 tablespoons hot milk
2 ½ cups flour
3 teaspoons baking powder

1 teaspoon cinnamon
1 teaspoon nutmeg
1 teaspoon vanilla
2 cups raw sweet potatoes,
   grated

Mix oil, sugar, beaten egg yolks, and hot milk. Sift flour, baking powder, cinnamon, nutmeg and salt. Stir; then add raw potatoes and flavoring. Beat until batter is smooth. Then beat egg whites stiff and fold into batter. Pour into greased cake pan. Bake at 350 degrees for 35-40 minutes.

TANGERINE RIND CAKE

3 eggs
1 ¼ cups sugar
½ cup butter
1 cup milk
2 ½ cups sifted cake flour

¼ teaspoon salt
2 teaspoons baking powder
¾ cup orange juice
¼ cup grated tangerine
   rind

Beat eggs, then add sugar, butter, milk, flour, salt, and baking powder. Beat batter until smooth, and add tangerine rind and orange juice. Pour into cake pan and bake at 350 degrees for 30 minutes or until done.

WHITE CAKE

6 egg whites
1 1/3 cups sugar
1/2 cup butter
1/4 teaspoon salt
3 cups cake flour

1 1/2 teaspoon baking
powder
1 1/4 cups milk
1 teaspoon vanilla

Mix ingredients: eggs, sugar, butter, salt; mix well. Add cake flour, baking powder, milk, and vanilla. Beat until batter is smooth. Bake at 350 degrees for 40 minutes. *Makes 2 layers.*

BANANA FILLING AND FROSTING

2 tablespoons cornstarch
3 tablespoons sugar
1 16-ounce can crushed
pineapple, undrained

1/2 box powdered sugar
1/4 cup margarine, melted
1 whole banana, mashed

Combine cornstarch, sugar and pineapple. Cook for 6 or 7 minutes; remove from heat. Cool and spread between layers of cake. Combine powdered sugar, melted margarine, and mashed banana. Mix well and spread on top layer of cake.

COCONUT AND PINEAPPLE TOPPING

1 16-ounce can vanilla
frosting
1 13-ounce can moist
coconut

1 15½-ounce crushed
pineapple, drained

Combine coconut and crushed pineapple. Place vanilla frosting on cake then add coconut and pineapple on each layer.

QUICK CARAMEL MILK ICING

2 cups brown sugar
1 teaspoon vanilla

¾ cup Pet milk
¼ cup margarine, melted

Dissolve brown sugar in melted margarine; add vanilla. Pour milk into a small pan and let milk come to a boil. Pour sugar and melted margarine in at once and continuously stir until thick and smooth. Remove from heat; let cool and spread on layer cake.

BROWN SUGAR COCONUT TOPPING

2 cups brown sugar
3¼ cups Pet milk
½ stick margarine

1 can (3½ ounces) coconut
flakes
1½ cups chopped pecans

In medium mixing bowl combine all ingredients and blend until smooth. Add milk and nuts last. Spread over 1 layer cake.

CARAMEL ICING

3½ cups sugar   ¾ cup milk
Pinch salt   ¼ cup butter
1 teaspoon butternut   1 tablespoon cornstarch
   vanilla flavoring

Let sugar brown lightly in butter; then pour into milk. Mix cornstarch with milk; let milk boil in a double boiler. Stir. Add flavoring
and a pinch of salt. Stir; cook until thick and smooth. Spread on
layer cake.

PEANUT BUTTER FROSTING

1 pound powdered sugar   ¼ cup Pet milk
2 teaspoons vanilla   1 cup peanut butter

Blend all ingredients together until smooth and spread. Will frost
1 layer cake.

LEMON ICING

2 cups powdered sugar   1 tablespoon margarine,
3 tablespoons milk   melted
2 teaspoons lemon juice   Yellow food color, optional

Blend ingredients together until smooth. If desired, add yellow
food color. Let cake cool before icing. Makes enough for one layer
cake.

HOLIDAY ICING

3 tablespoons milk
½ cup melted margarine

½ box powdered sugar
2 tablespoons brandy

Mix margarine, sugar, milk and stir. Add brandy and stir until smooth. Frosts 1 layer cake.

PET MILK FROSTING

1 box powdered sugar
1 small can Pet milk
¼ cup margarine

2 teaspoons vanilla
    flavoring

Mix all ingredients together. Stir until smooth and spread on layer cake.

PINEAPPLE FROSTING

3 cups sugar
¼ cup butter
2 tablespoons cornstarch
1 cup Pet milk

2 teaspoons pineapple
    flavoring
1 teaspoon lemon juice

Blend ingredients all together. Stir until smooth and spread.

Pies

APPLE PIE

3 cups apples
2 tablespoons water
½ cup margarine
½ teaspoon cinnamon
1½ cups sugar

¼ teaspoon nutmeg
1 teaspoon applespice
2 tablespoons cornstarch
Double crust pie pastry

Peel and slice apples. Put apples into a small pot with water, margarine, sugar, cinnamon, nutmeg, and applespice. Cook until well done. Remove from heat and stir in cornstarch. Pour apples into crust. Strip top of pie with thin dough. Sprinkle sugar and cinnamon over top crust and dot with butter. Bake in oven at 375 degrees for 45 minutes. If desired, serve with ice cream on top.

BANANA PIE

3 egg yolks
¾ cup sugar
4 tablespoons butter
¼ teaspoon salt
2 cups milk

2 tablespoons cornstarch
2 large bananas, mashed
1 teaspoon vanilla
1 graham cracker crust

Mix eggs, sugar, butter, milk and salt; stir until smooth. Add cornstarch; cook over medium heat until thick. Remove from heat; add mashed bananas and vanilla. Pour into graham cracker crust. Top with meringue and brown in oven.

COUNTRY BLACKBERRY PIE

2 pints fresh blackberries
1 quart water
2 tablespoons flour
2 cups sugar

½ cup margarine
Pinch salt
Double crust pie pastry

Wash berries. Put into pan and add 1 quart cold water and cook until tender. Stir in flour, sugar, butter and salt. Cook until mixture becomes thick. Pour into crust; strip top with crust. Sprinkle sugar over crust and dot with butter. Bake at 350 degrees for 30 minutes.

COCOA CHESS PIE

½ cup butter
2 tablespoons cocoa
2½ cups sugar
2 eggs

⅔ cup Pet milk
1½ teaspoons vanilla
1 pie pastry, unbaked

Melt butter and mix with cocoa and sugar. Add eggs, milk and vanilla; beat until smooth. Pour into crust and bake at 350 degrees for 30 or 40 minutes.

QUICK CHOCOLATE ICE BOX PIE

2 boxes 3½-ounce Jello
   chocolate instant
   pudding
2¾ cups cold milk

1 teaspoon vanilla
   flavoring
1 graham cracker crust
Whipped topping

Mix ingredients until smooth, pour into graham cracker crust. Top with Dream Whip or Cool Whip and chill 1 hour before serving.

COCONUT CREAM PIE

4 egg yolks
1¾ cups sugar
¼ cup butter
Pinch salt
3 tablespoons cornstarch

3 cups milk
1 teaspoon vanilla
1 small can coconut cream
1 pie shell, baked

Place beaten egg yolks, sugar, butter and salt in top of a double boiler. Dissolve cornstarch in milk, then add vanilla and coconut cream and combine with other ingredients. Stir over medium heat until thick and smooth. Pour filling into already baked crust; top with meringue and brown in preheated oven 30 minutes at 350 degrees.

CHERRY PIE

2 cans cherry pie filling
⅓ cup sugar
3 tablespoons margarine,
   melted

1 teaspoon vanilla or
   almond extract
1 double crust pie pastry

Mix cherries, sugar, margarine and extract; stir together. Pour into pie crust; strip top with dough. Bake at 350 degrees for 25 to 30 minutes.

CHESS PIE

3 eggs
1½ cups sugar
¼ cup brown sugar
2 tablespoons flour

Pinch salt
3 tablespoons milk
1 teaspoon vanilla
½ cup margarine, melted

Beat eggs, sugars, flour, salt, milk, vanilla and margarine. Stir until smooth; pour into unbaked pie crust. Bake at 350 degrees for 30 minutes.

APPLE COBBLER

8 apples, sliced   1 teaspoon applespice
1 quart water   1 teaspoon cinnamon
2 cups sugar   Dash salt
1 stick butter   1 tablespoon cornstarch

Peel and slice apples. Place in a pan with water, sugar, butter and spices. Add dash of salt. Stir in cornstarch and pour into a 2 quart dish on top of Crazy Crust and cook 25-30 minutes at 350 degrees. *Good with ice cream.*

BLACKBERRY COBBLER

2 16-ounce cans   1 tablespoon cornstarch
   blackberries   2½ cups sugar
1 stick butter   1 can cold water

Pour berries and water into saucepan. Add butter and sugar; stir in cornstarch. Cook until slightly thick. Remove from heat. Pour into casserole dish on Crazy Crust or roll thin crust and place crust on bottom and top of cobbler. Dot with butter. Sprinkle with sugar. Put into oven and brown at 350 degrees for 45 minutes. Serve with your favorite ice cream.

PEACH COBBLER

2 16-ounce cans sliced
   peaches
1 ½ cups sugar
1 stick butter

1 tablespoon cornstarch
1 teaspoon vanilla
1 can biscuits, optional

Combine peaches, sugar, butter and cornstarch. Cook over medium heat until mixture begins to get thick. Remove from heat. Add vanilla. Pour peaches into pan on Crazy Crust or use can biscuits rolled very thin and place on bottom and top of cobbler. Sprinkle top with sugar and dots of butter. Bake until brown at 375 degrees for 25 to 30 minutes.

FRUIT COCKTAIL AND PEAR COBBLER

1 17-ounce can fruit
   cocktail
1 15½-ounce can pears
1 tablespoon cornstarch
1 teaspoon nutmeg

1 teaspoon ground cloves
1 teaspoon vanilla
2 tablespoons margarine
⅔ cup sugar

Pour fruit cocktail into a large bowl. Cut pears into small pieces. Mix cornstarch in syrup from fruit. Add nutmeg, ground cloves, vanilla, and melted butter and sugar. Pour into casserole dish over Crazy Crust. Bake at 400 degrees for 25 to 30 minutes.

PEAR COBBLER

5 cups pears
⅓ cup butter
1 teaspoon applespice

1 teaspoon nutmeg
2 teaspoons cornstarch
1 tablespoon lemon juice

Cook pears until tender. Combine butter, applespice, and nutmeg. Stir cornstarch in a little water and mix into pears. Cook for 5 minutes. Remove from heat; stir in lemon juice. Pour pears into dish on top of Crazy Crust and bake at 350 degrees for 25 minutes. Serve warm or cold.

CRAZY CRUST FOR COBBLER

1 cup self-rising flour
1 cup sugar

1 stick butter
⅔ cup milk

Combine all ingredients. Stir until smooth. Pour into cobbler dish over fruit of your choice. During the cooking the batter will come to the top and make crust. Bake at 350 degrees for 45 minutes to 1 hour.

GREEN MOUNTAIN ICE BOX PIE

1 can Eagle Brand milk
Juice of 2 lemons
1 cup coconut cream
1 can crushed pineapple

½ cup cherries, sliced in half
½ cup nuts, finely chopped
1 large box Cool Whip
1 graham cracker crust

Blend milk, lemon juice, coconut cream, pineapple, cherries, and chopped nuts. Fold Cool Whip into fruit and milk. Pour into graham cracker crust. If desired, sprinkle nuts over top of pie. Chill until ready to serve.

LEMON CHIFFON PIE

3 egg yolks (reserve whites
   for meringue)
1 cup milk
Pinch salt
¼ cup grated lemon rind

1¾ cup sugar
Juice of 3 lemons
1 envelope unflavored
   gelatin
1 pre-baked pastry shell

Combine all ingredients and place in top of a double boiler. Cook until thick and creamy, stirring often. Pour into crust.

Meringue

3 egg whites
½ teaspoon vanilla

¼ cup powdered sugar
½ teaspoon cream of tartar

Beat egg whites until stiff peaks are formed. Add vanilla, sugar, and cream of tartar. Spread over top of pie. Bake enough to brown meringue about 3 minutes at 400 degrees.

EGG CUSTARD PIE

6 eggs
¼ teaspoon salt
1⅓ cups milk

¾ cups sugar
¼ cup butter
1 teaspoon vanilla

Beat eggs, sugar, milk, butter, salt; mix well. Add vanilla. Stir until smooth and pour into pie crust. Bake at 300 degrees for 45 minutes.

LEMON ICE BOX PIE

Juice of 3 lemons
1 can sweetened condensed
   milk

1 teaspoon vanilla
1 9-inch graham cracker
   crust

Mix well the lemon juice and condensed milk until smooth and creamy. Add vanilla; stir again. Pour into graham cracker crust. Sprinkle some graham cracker crumbs over top of pie. Chill until ready to serve.

LEMON MERINGUE PIE

Filling

1 ¼ cups sugar
3 tablespoons cornstarch
1 ¼ cups water
Dash salt
2 tablespoons margarine

3 egg yolks
Juice of 3 lemons
1 teaspoon vanilla
1 9-inch pie crust

Mix sugar, cornstarch, salt, margarine and water together in top of a double boiler. Cook 3 to 5 minutes over medium heat. Beat egg yolks; then add to previous ingredients. Remove from heat; stir in lemon juice and vanilla. Pour into 9-inch pie crust. Bake at 350 degrees for 20 to 40 minutes.

Meringue

3 egg whites
¼ teaspoon cream of tartar

¼ cup powdered sugar
1 teaspoon vanilla

Add cream of tartar to egg whites. Beat egg whites until stiff. Fold in powdered sugar and vanilla. Top pie and bake 10 minutes longer until light brown.

MERINGUE

3 egg whites
1 cup confectioners sugar

1 teaspoon vanilla
Pinch baking powder

Beat egg whites until stiff peaks are formed; then add powdered sugar, vanilla and baking powder. Spread over pies. Let meringue brown lightly in 400 degree oven for 3 to 4 minutes. Remove pie from oven; cool and serve.

EASY MINCEMEAT PIE

1 18-ounce jar mincemeat
1 teaspoon applespice
2 cups diced apples

¼ cup butter
Double crust pie pastry

Combine all ingredients in a bowl. Pour mixture into pie crust. Strip top with dough. Bake at 350 degrees for 40 to 45 minutes.

MOCK MINCE-APPLE PIE

3 tablespoons butter
⅔ cup brown sugar
⅓ cup self-rising flour
Pinch salt
⅓ cup water
2 teaspons cinnamon
1 teaspoon applespice

¼ grated orange peel
¼ cup chopped candied
 dates
1½ cups diced apples
¼ cup brandy
Powdered sugar
Double crust pie pastry

Combine butter, sugar, flour, salt, warm water, spices and fruit. Beat until smooth; add brandy last. Pour filling into bottom of crust. Cover with top crust and seal edges. Make a few slits in top crust to allow steam to escape. Sprinkle top with powdered sugar. Bake at 400 degrees for 35 to 40 minutes.

FRIED PEACH PIE

1 package dried peaches
3 cups water
1 teaspoon vanilla
2 cups sugar

1 teaspoon cinnamon
½ cup shortening or
 cooking oil
Pie pastry

Soak peaches in cold water overnight and cook in the same water for flavor. Cook until tender; mash peaches and sweeten to own taste. Add cinnamon, vanilla and remainder of sugar if needed. Cut pastry dough in squares or circles about 6 inches in diameter; then place the amount of peaches you want in each pie on the pastry. Fold over and press edges together with a fork. Fry in hot oil until brown on both sides.

PEANUT BUTTER PIE

½ cup sugar
¾ cup powdered sugar
Dash salt
1 junket tablet
1 tablespoon cornstarch
2 cups milk

1 cup peanut butter
1 teaspoon vanilla
3 egg yolks, beaten
Pie pastry
2 or 3 bananas

Mix sugars and salt together. Dissolve junket tablet and corn-starch in 1 cup milk. Stir in peanut butter, vanilla, eggs, and remaining cup of milk. Pour peanut butter mixture into a light brown crust and bake at 300 degrees for 45 minutes. Top pie with mashed bananas before serving.

PECAN PIE

2 teaspoons flour
⅔ cups brown sugar
1½ cups dark corn syrup
4 eggs
¼ teaspoon salt

2 teaspoons vanilla
¼ cup butter
1 cup pecan halves
1 9-inch unbaked pie pastry

Combine flour, brown sugar, corn syrup, eggs, salt, vanilla; mix well, then stir in butter and pecans. Pour into 9-inch pie crust. Bake at 375 degrees for 35 or 45 minutes until golden brown.

PECAN TASSIES

Crust

1 3-ounce package cream
cheese, softened

½ cup butter, softened
¾ cup flour

Blend cream cheese and butter together. Stir in flour and shape into balls. Press a ball of dough into each cup of a muffin pan so that you have what looks like miniature pie shells. Bake filled pastry for 30 minutes at 325 degrees.

Filling

1 teaspoon vanilla extract
Dash salt
1 egg

¾ cup brown sugar
¼ cup chopped pecans

Combine egg, chopped nuts, salt, brown sugar, and vanilla. Pour filling into pastry shells.

PIE CRUST

2½ cups all-purpose flour
¹/₈ teaspoon baking powder
1 teaspoon salt

½ cup Crisco shortening
⅔ cup sweet milk

Pour flour into a large bowl and add salt and baking powder. Mix in Crisco shortening with a pastry blender. Pour milk in gradually and mix after each addition. Work dough over and over in flour until not sticky; place on floured board. Roll dough out ¼-inch thick. Place into pie pan.

PINEAPPLE-SWEET POTATO PIE

3 or 4 large sweet potatoes
¼ cup Pet milk
2 teaspoons vanilla
½ cup butter, melted

3 eggs, beaten
1½ cups sugar
1 small can crushed
   pineapple, drained

Boil sweet potatoes in clear water until tender. Peel potatoes while warm, put into a large bowl and mash. Stir in remainder of ingredients. Pour into unbaked pie crust. Bake at 350 degrees for 45 minutes until light brown.

SOUR CREAM PIE

1 small box vanilla instant
   pudding
1½ cups cold milk
Pinch salt

1 cup dairy sour cream
1 teaspoon vanilla extract
1 graham cracker crust
Whipped cream

Pour instant vanilla pudding into a large bowl; add milk and salt. Stir until smooth. Stir in sour cream and vanilla. Pour into graham cracker crust. Top with whipped cream. Chill 1 hour before serving.

RAISIN PIE

2 boxes white raisins
2½ cups water
2 tablespoons cornstarch
2 cups sugar

3 tablespoons lemon juice
¼ cup margarine
1 9-inch pie crust

Simmer raisins in water for 25 minutes. Dissolve cornstarch in ¼ cup water; add sugar. Pour into raisins; stir. Add lemon juice and margarine. Pour into pie crust; strip top with dough. Bake at 350 degrees for 35-40 minutes.

PUMPKIN PIE

1 16-ounce can pumpkin
   pie filling
3 eggs
1½ cups sugar
1⅔ cup milk
½ cup margarine

Pinch salt
1 teaspoon cinnamon
1 teaspoon pumpkinspice
1 unbaked pie shell

Beat ingredients until smooth. Pour filling into pie crust and bake in a preheated oven at 350 degrees for 30 to 35 minutes or until lightly browned.

PRUNE PIE

1 box Del-Monte prunes
3 cups water
½ cup margarine

1 ½ cups sugar
2 ½ tablespoons cornstarch
1 pie crust

Soak prunes overnight in water. Cook prunes in water in which they were soaked. Add sugar; cook until tender. Add margarine; stir in cornstarch. Pour into pie crust. Sprinkle with a little sugar and dots of butter. Place strips of dough on top of pie. Bake at 375 for 25 to 30 minutes.

Desserts

VANILLA ICE CREAM

1 gallon milk
6 eggs
3½ cups sugar
Pinch salt

2 teaspoons vanilla
 flavoring
1 junket tablet

Cook milk over medium heat in top of a double boiler. Beat eggs; pour into milk. Mix sugar, salt and vanilla. Dissolve junket tablet in ¼ cup warm milk and add to custard. Pour into ice cream freezer and freeze.

NO COOK PINEAPPLE ICE CREAM

2 cans Eagle Brand milk
3 quarts sweet milk
6 eggs, separated

2 teaspoons vanilla
1 large can crushed
 pineapple

Combine Eagle Brand milk and sweet milk. Beat egg yolks well; add vanilla and crushed pineapple. Beat egg whites to soft peak stage. Fold into custard and freeze. *Makes 1 gallon.*

TWELVE FLAVOR ICE CREAM DESSERT

1 scoop each:
Vanilla ice cream
Pineapple sherbet
Black walnut ice cream
Banana split ice cream
Lime sherbet
Orange sherbet
Butter pecan ice cream

Strawberry ice cream
Chocolate chip ice cream
Black cherry ice cream
Lemon ice cream
Peach ice cream
1 pint fresh strawberries

This is a combination of different kinds of ice cream. Mix together in a large bowl. Center on the table for dessert with fresh strawberries on top. Serve with chocolate chip cookies. *Some days this is all Elvis would have during the day.*

OLD FASHIONED BREAD PUDDING

12 biscuits
2 cups milk
2 eggs

½ cup butter
1½ cups sugar
2 teaspoons vanilla

Crumble biscuits then pour milk into crumbs. Add egg, butter, sugar and vanilla. Beat until smooth then pour into greased pan. Bake until lightly browned about 1 to 1½ hours at 325 degrees.

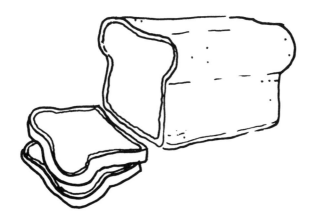

RICE PUDDING

5 cups cooked rice
1 tablespoon flour
2½ cups milk
1½ cups sugar

8 tablespoons butter
4 eggs
1¼ teaspoons vanilla
½ cup seedless raisins

Mix cooked rice, flour and milk over low heat. Combine eggs, sugar and melted butter. Beat; then add flavoring and raisins. Pour into greased pan. Bake at 350 degrees for 40 minutes. *Serves 4.*

SWEET POTATO PUDDING

4 or 5 sweet potatoes,
  cooked
½ cup butter
2 eggs
1½ cups sugar
1 teaspoon nutmeg

1 teaspoon vanilla
⅓ cup flour
½ cup milk
1 small can crushed
  pineapple

Peel potatoes and mash. Add butter, egg, sugar, nutmeg, and vanilla flavoring. Add flour and milk; stir in crushed pineapple. Pour into a greased pan and cook 25 to 30 minutes at 350 degrees. If desired, put 4 or 5 marshmallows on top.

PEPPERMINT ICE CREAM

2 quarts milk
3 eggs
2 cups sugar
⅛ teaspoon salt
1 junket rennet tablet

¼ cup warm water
2 teaspoons vanilla
1 small package crushed
  peppermint candy

Dissolve junket tablet in lukewarm water. In top of a double boiler, combine eggs and milk. Add sugar and salt; stir; cook for 3 minutes. Add dissolved junket tablet, vanilla and crushed peppermint candy. Stir and freeze in ice cream freezer.

PUDDING SAUCE

½ cup butter

1 egg

3 tablespoons lemon juice

1 cup powdered sugar

2 teaspoons vanilla

Pinch salt

Melt butter; add sugar. Beat egg with rotary beater. Cook in a double boiler; stir in other ingredients until thick. Cool and serve with cake.

BANANA PUDDING

6 eggs, separated

3 cups milk

1¼ cups sugar

3 tablespoons cornstarch

Dash salt

2 teaspoons vanilla

5 or 6 bananas, sliced

Vanilla wafers

Cream of tartar

¼ cup powdered sugar

Beat egg yolks; pour into milk. Stir in sugar and cornstarch and salt; cook in a double boiler. Stir constantly to keep from lumping. Cook until smooth and thick; remove from heat. Add vanilla. Make layer of vanilla wafers and bananas in dish then pour part of the custard; make another layer of wafers and bananas and custard. Beat egg whites until stiff. Add pinch of cream of tartar and powdered sugar. Spread over top. Bake in 400 degree oven for 5 to 7 minutes until lightly browned.

BAKED APPLE AND SWEET POTATO PUDDING

4 large sweet potatoes	½ teaspoon cinnamon
3 medium apples	1 teaspoon applespice
1 cup water	½ cup of butter, melted
½ cup brown sugar	½ teaspoon vanilla

Wash; peel sweet potatoes and apples. Cut into slices. Cover bottom of pan with graham cracker crumbs. Layer potatoes and apples in dish. Mix brown sugar with water and pour over each layer. Season each layer with cinnamon, applespice, butter, and flavoring. Spread a few graham cracker crumbs over the top. Bake at 350 degrees for 45 minutes. Let pudding stand for 4 or 5 minutes, then serve.

STRAWBERRY DESSERT

1 pint fresh strawberries	1½ cups sugar
1 cup Cool Whip	Graham crackers

Pick fresh strawberries, rinse, place in a bowl. Add sugar and chill strawberries until ready to serve. Top with Cool Whip. Serve with graham crackers on the side.

BROWNIES

3 squares unsweetened
   chocolate
1 egg
1 cup sugar
1 teaspoon vanilla

½ cup pecans, chopped
1 ¼ cup flour
¼ cup melted butter
Dash salt
1 teaspoon baking powder

Melt chocolate in saucepan over low heat. Combine other ingredients. Stir into chocolate. Mix well. Pour into greased pan. Bake at 350 degrees for 25 to 30 minutes. Cut into squares and serve.

CREAM PUFFS

1 cup hot water
½ cup butter
1 ½ cups self-rising flour

4 eggs
3 cups whipped cream

Add butter to boiling water; then the flour, stirring constantly. Cook over direct heat for 15 minutes. Remove from heat. Add unbeaten eggs one at a time. Stir well. Drop spoonful of batter onto baking sheet. Allow 2 to 3 inches between for expansion. Bake at 450 degrees for 15 minutes. Reduce heat to 350 degrees and bake 25 to 30 minutes more. Let cool; split open and fill with whipped cream. *Makes 12 puffs.*

QUICK PINEAPPLE DESSERT

1 20-ounce can crushed
  pineapple
½ cup sugar
2 tablespoons cornstarch
¼ cup margarine

2 eggs
1 cup Pet milk
½ teaspoon cinnamon
1 teaspoon vanilla
1 graham cracker crust

Mix crushed pineapple, sugar, cornstarch, margarine, eggs, milk, cinnamon, and flavoring. Stir altogether. Cook over low heat until it starts to thicken. Remove from heat. Pour into graham cracker crust. Sprinkle some crumbs over top of pie. Chill for 2 hours.

SPICED PEAR DESSERT

2 16-ounce cans pears
1½ cups cold water
2 tablespons cornstarch
½ cup butter
1½ cups sugar
1 teaspoon ginger
2 teaspoons cinnamon

¼ teaspoon nutmeg
1 teaspoon ground cloves
3 tablespoons lemon juice
¼ cup sherry cooking wine
1 graham cracker crust
Cool Whip

Cook pears over medium heat. Add cold water then cornstarch, butter, sugar, and spices. Stir; cook until thick. Remove from heat. Add wine and lemon juice last. Pour into graham cracker crust. Let it cool. Top with Cool Whip. Chill for 30 minutes before serving. Keep in refrigerator.

PECAN PUFFS

2 cups light brown sugar
1 teaspoon vanilla
2 egg whites

1 cup unbroken pecan
  halves

Beat egg whites until stiff; add sugar, vanilla, and pecans. Drop from spoon onto greased cookie sheet. Bake at 250 degrees for 25 minutes.

ORANGE-SWEET POTATO DESSERT

2 17-ounce cans yams
1 teaspoon vanilla
½ cup brown sugar
⅓ cup margarine

Grated peel of 4 oranges
⅔ cup miniature
    marshmallows

Pour yams into a 1-quart pan; add vanilla, brown sugar, margarine, finely grated orange peel and stir into yams. Cook in oven for 20 minutes at 350 degrees; then add marshmallows on top and cook for 3 minutes until brown. Cool and serve.

RED JELLO DIET DESSERT

5 cans strawberry Shasta
    drinks
4½ packages Sweet-n-Low

15 envelopes Knox gelatin
2 tablespoons banana
    flavoring

Boil Shasta in kettle until it bubbles. Pour hot Shasta into a large bowl and stir in Sweet-n-Low, banana flavoring, and gelatin. Stir. Pour into a 2-quart dish and chill. Cut into squares and serve.

APPLESAUCE TURNOVERS

2 cups pancake mix
1 egg
1 cup milk

1½ cups applesauce
1 teaspoon applespice
Pinch salt

Combine pancake mix into bowl with egg, milk, applesauce, applespice and pinch of salt. Beat batter until smooth. Pour into hot oil and brown. Serve immediately.

Beverages

APPLE PEEL WINE

1 gallon water
3 yeast cakes
5 pounds sugar

1 quart orange juice
Juice of 3 medium lemons
Peeling from 12 tart apples

Bring water to a boil. Dissolve yeast cakes in boiling water. Stir in sugar, orange juice, lemon juice and apple peeling. Remove from heat; pour into a large jug but do not fill completely to top. Do not tighten lid on jug. Let peeling and juices stand for 9 days. Strain and sweeten to taste. Good for holidays.

TIPSEY EGGNOG

6 eggs, well beaten
1 gallon milk
1 ½ cups sugar
2 junket tablets

2 teaspoons nutmeg
2 teaspoons vanilla
⅓ cup whiskey
Pinch salt

Beat eggs well, add milk and sugar to own taste, and dissolve junket tablets in ¼ cup warm water. Stir. Add junket, nutmeg and vanilla to milk and cook until smooth and thick in double boiler. Add salt, whiskey, and chill until ready to serve.

GINGER ALE PUNCH

1 ½ cups water
½ cup sugar
4 sticks cinnamon
5 cans frozen orange juice

1 quart cherry juice
1 quart pineapple juice
1 cup cherries
1 quart ginger ale

Place water, sugar, and cinnamon in saucepan over high heat. Bring to a boil, stirring to dissolve sugar. Boil 5 minutes. Remove from heat and strain. Stir syrup into other juices. Mix well and chill until ready to serve. Add ginger ale and cherries just before serving. *Serves 12.*

May add rum to punch if desired.

PUNCH

1 quart Lipton tea   1 cup sugar
1 quart pineapple juice   3 oranges
1 quart lemonade

Make tea and sweeten with sugar. Add lemonade, pineapple juice; stir well. Rinse oranges and thinly slice. Do not peel. Cut orange slices in half and add to punch. Chill well. Serve in large punch bowl. *Makes 12 servings.*

May add 1 can of Hawaiian Punch fruit juice if desired.

EGG NOG

10 eggs, beaten   4 cups sugar
½ teaspoon salt   1 gallon milk
2 teaspoons nutmeg   2 tablespoons cornstarch
2 teaspoons vanilla

Cook over medium heat in a double boiler. Stir constantly to keep from lumping. Gradually add beaten eggs. Stir in nutmeg, vanilla and salt. Mix cornstarch in a little milk before adding to make egg nog thick. Cook until smooth. If not thick enough, add more cornstarch. Remove from heat and cool. Add your favorite whiskey. Chill and serve.

ELVIS' FAVORITE DRINKS

SOFT DRINKS
Dr. Pepper
Orange Crush
Pepsi Cola
Root Beer
Grape Drink
Peach Drink
RC Cola
Mountain Dew

DIET DRINKS
Strawberry Shasta
Creme Soda
Black Cherry Shasta
Raspberry Shasta
Grape Shasta

JUICES
Orange juice
Grape juice
Apple juice
Gatorade

OTHER DRINKS
Tonic water
Ice water
Mountain Valley Water
Coffee / cream / Sweet N Low
Sweet milk
Bulghar buttermilk

Elvis always wanted to drink ice water at each meal. All of these other drinks were served at different times, depending on what he wanted.

Index

A
ACCOMPANIMENTS

APPETIZERS

APPLE

B

BANANA

BEANS

BEEF

BEVERAGES

BREADS

The Presley Family Cookbook
Wimmer Cookbook Distribution
4650 Shelby Air Drive
Memphis, Tennessee 38118

Please send me _____ copies   @ $13.95 each _____
Tennessee residents add sales tax   @   1.36 each _____
Postage and handling   @ $ 6.00 each _____

Name_____

Address_____

City_____ State_____ Zip_____

To order by Visa or MasterCard call 1-800-548-2537

- -

The Presley Family Cookbook
Wimmer Cookbook Distribution
4650 Shelby Air Drive
Memphis, Tennessee 38118

Please send me _____ copies   @ $13.95 each _____
Tennessee residents add sales tax   @   1.36 each _____
Postage and handling   @ $ 6.00 each _____

Name_____

Address_____

City_____ State_____ Zip_____

To order by Visa or MasterCard call 1-800-548-2537

- -

The Presley Family Cookbook
Wimmer Cookbook Distribution
4650 Shelby Air Drive
Memphis, Tennessee 38118

Please send me _____ copies   @ $13.95 each _____
Tennessee residents add sales tax   @   1.36 each _____
Postage and handling   @ $ 6.00 each _____

Name_____

Address_____

City_____ State_____ Zip_____

To order by Visa or MasterCard call 1-800-548-2537

Save $1.00 on your reorder. Just send us the name, address, and phone number of the best stores in your town that sell cookbooks.

Name of Store _____

Owner or Managers Name _____

Address _____

City_____ State_____ Zip_____
(Deduct $1.00 off your reorder when this is filled in)

|||||||||||||||||||||||||||||||||||||||||||||||||||||||||||||||||||||||||||||||||||||||||||||||||||||||||||||

Save $1.00 on your reorder. Just send us the names and addresses of two of your friends that collect cookbooks.

1   Name _____

    Address _____

    City_____ State_____ Zip_____

2   Name _____

    Address _____

    City_____ State_____ Zip_____
(Deduct $1.00 off your reorder when this is filled in)

|||||||||||||||||||||||||||||||||||||||||||||||||||||||||||||||||||||||||||||||||||||||||||||||||||||||||||||

Save $1.00 on your reorder. Just send us the name, address, and phone number of the best stores in your town that sell cookbooks.

Name of Store _____

Owner or Managers Name _____

Address _____

City_____ State_____ Zip_____
(Deduct $1.00 off your reorder when this is filled in)